Date Due

DANGEROUS LEGACY

DANGEROUS LEGACY
THE BABIES OF
DRUG-TAKING PARENTS

BEN SONDER

FRANKLIN WATTS
NEW YORK / CHICAGO / LONDON / TORONTO / SYDNEY

Library of Congress Cataloging-in-Publication Data

Sonder, Ben. 1954–
    Dangerous Legacy: the babies of drug-taking parents / Ben Sonder
    p. cm.
    Includes bibliographical references (p.   ) and index.
    ISBN 0-531-11195-4 (lib. bdg.)
    1. Children of narcotic addicts — United States — Juvenile
literature. 2. Children of alcoholics — United States — Juvenile
literature. 3. Tobacco — Physiological effect — Juvenile literature.
[1. Drug abuse. 2. Alcoholism. 3. Smoking. 4. Parent and child.]
I. Title
HV5824.C45s66 1994
362.29'13'0973—dc20   94-15076 CIP AC

CONTENTS

DANGEROUS LEGACY

A NOTE ABOUT THE TITLE

THIS BOOK was originally to be titled *Drug Babies*. However, research on the subject of babies whose parents took drugs before, during, and after pregnancy revealed the bias in the term *drug baby*. At the beginning of the American crack epidemic of the mid-1980s, the label *drug baby* was applied to newborns whose mothers took drugs and who had neurological, behavioral, and other problems. Most researchers at the time thought these were permanent birth defects and that children born with them would always suffer severely. Current research reveals grounds for optimism. Educators, physicians, and caring parents have discovered that many of the children who had been labeled "drug babies" can go on to lead normal lives. Researchers have found that their behavioral and learning problems sometimes disappear as they grow older. They may have been born "drug babies," but they are not "drug children."

Another reason not to use the term is that these children, unlike most people who are harmed by drugs, did not choose to put them in their bodies. Their only association with drugs was caused by the action of others. Thus, the term *drug baby* makes about as much sense as calling an abused child a *"violence child."* The violence is in the adult who inflicts it, not in the child. Drugs that affect very young children are a legacy they inherit from their parents — but not an unescapable one. Some of the supposed doomed "drug babies" of the 1980s have become the normal children of today.

CHAPTER 1

THE SPECIAL CASE OF DRUGS IN AMERICA

TIME: 1886

PLACE: Somewhere in America

NAME: "Elizabeth"

OCCUPATION: Housewife[1]

"ELIZABETH" was a new bride in late-nineteenth-century America who suffered from severe depression. Her doctor prescribed a miracle drug, then used by some progressive physicians for problems of depression or lack of energy. It was called cocaine. After her first dose of the substance, Elizabeth's condition improved greatly. She eventually discovered she was pregnant. During Elizabeth's entire pregnancy, she used the drug whenever she felt "down."

The story of the effects of drugs on adults and children is as old as childbearing itself. Human beings have always taken intoxicants. An *intoxicant* is a substance that changes the functioning of the nervous system, either exciting or depressing it. Intoxicants can affect a person's sensory, thinking, or emotive patterns. Alcohol is a legal intoxicant in the United States, but marijuana, cocaine, and heroin are intoxicants as well. In large doses, intoxicants can kill a person. In fact, the word *intoxicant* is derived from the Latin word *toxicum*, meaning poison.

In almost every society and in every century, intoxicants have been used in religious rituals, at festivals, or at the dinner table. They were consumed by men, by both pregnant and nonpregnant women, and even by children. Alcohol is a good example of an intoxicant that has played an important social role in Western culture for centuries. Wine has been a common table beverage since the time of the classical Greeks. In ancient Greece, then later in Europe and colonial America, the whole family drank wine daily at table. Since it was fermented and did not contaminate easily, it was often safer to drink than water. Though this beverage was always in danger of being abused, it was considered useful and even healthful when drunk sparingly and in the right situations.

For centuries alcohol has also been consumed as part of religious rituals. The Greeks and the Hebrews used wine in offerings and sacrifices. Then, several centuries later, Christians began using wine as part of their sacrament. The use of intoxicants for religious purposes occurs worldwide and in a variety of civilizations.

Among some South American tribal communities, the leaf of the coca plant, from which cocaine is derived, is chewed to provide energy during strenuous work or long marches. Chewing the leaf supplies a person with a much lower dose of pure cocaine than sniffing, injecting, or smoking the refined drug does. This long-standing tradition of chewing the coca leaf rarely leads to abuse of the plant. No one in the community believes the practice is harmful.

When an intoxicant is used for religious reasons or its use is strictly defined by custom, the potential for abusing it seems to decrease. The effect of the intoxicant may be pleasurable, but its main purpose is to enhance spiritual experience or to strengthen the social bonds of a community. Taking drugs in this context rarely leads to crime or antisocial behavior.

Some strong intoxicants have also been associated in the past with serious scientific experiments and philosophical quests. The writer Aldous Huxley experimented with the hallucinogenic drug mescaline during a ten-year period beginning in 1953, and he wrote about the visions he had under the influence of this drug. Sigmund Freud, the father of psychoanalysis, personally took cocaine as a painkiller, and wrote about its potential for treating some illnesses.

The very bad reputation of some drugs is a fairly recent one. How, then, did drug experimentation and habitual drug use change in quality, reach such dangerous proportions, and become linked with criminal behavior in contemporary America? The use of drugs in the past was strictly controlled by ritual, custom, scholarly inquiry, or the necessities of diet. Perhaps the abuse began when drug taking and drinking left traditional contexts and became a means of escape or self-gratification.

Some of the drugs being abused today were originally introduced into society by the medical profession. They were widely prescribed before scientists and physicians understood their potential for abuse. Many people became addicted or suffered health problems as a result of these practices.

In the nineteenth century, cocaine elixirs, teas, powders, and even soft drinks were recommended by many American and European doctors for such ailments as depression, lack of energy, hay fever, and some of the psychological problems of pregnancy. Until after World War I, cocaine and cocaine derivatives could be obtained at most pharmacies.[2] They were also added to some common household beverages. Even the original formula of Coca-Cola contained cocaine because of its invigorating effect upon the nervous system.

Opiates—drugs containing or derived from opium—such as morphine and codeine, which are highly addictive painkillers, were freely prescribed by American doctors between 1870 and 1916 for sleeplessness, migraines, back pain, and other less serious problems. At first, these opiates were not thought to be very dangerous, but then doctors began to notice that people developed dependence on them. Alarming withdrawal symptoms occurred in patients when the medication was stopped. Finally, government food and drug control agencies were organized, and both cocaine and opiates were placed under tight controls and administered only for serious ailments.

The 1960s ushered in a time of widespread uncontrolled experimentation with intoxicants. After a period of conformity in the 1950s, young people coming of age in the 1960s began to question many traditional beliefs. Conventional marriages and the family came under attack. The pursuit of pleasure became a highly valued activity. There was time and money for this obsession with pleasure. Most of the young people who led the sixties counterculture rebellion came from fairly well-to-do households. They hadn't faced economic uncertainty during the Depression or a world war as their parents or grandparents had. They were in no hurry to settle down, and many were not concerned with job security or the pressures of maintaining a family.

The rebellious, free-thinking hippies of the sixties and seventies were also extremely interested in intoxicants. Drug taking fit in perfectly with the emphasis on pleasure, quick results, and a lifestyle cleansed of conventional responsibilities. Until the 1960s, only alcohol and opiates had been abused on a large scale in the United States. Hallucinogens such as marijuana or hashish were popular in some small subcultures found in urban ghettoes or the jazz circles of New York's Greenwich Village. But in the 1960s these drugs—as well as the stronger hallucinogens LSD, mescaline, and psilocybin—were brought into the mainstream of society.

The new drug culture of the sixties began with an attempt to place drug taking in an ideal and meaningful context. The first people to promote the use of hallucinogens were educated people like Timothy Leary, a Harvard psychology professor who saw hallucinogens as aids to achieving psychological or spiritual insights. In advocating use of these drugs, Leary and others cited the studies of Aldous Huxley and the rituals of some Native American tribes, who chewed the hallucinogenic peyote root (containing mescaline) to achieve religious visions. The elated experiences Leary and others had under the influence of these drugs were compared to the egoless state achieved by Eastern mystics.

Thus, drug taking in the sixties began partly with an attempt to place drugs in a positive context—the context of religion and spirituality. However, this attempt to create new spiritual values in America with the aid of drugs never succeeded. It is one thing to be a member of a tightly knit Native American community in which certain revered rituals using hallucinogens play a profound part. It is another thing to try to create a new spiritual culture by oneself. The people who began taking drugs were neither Sioux Indians nor disciplined intellectuals like Aldous Huxley. Before long, drug taking had lost its claims to spiritual awareness and had simply become a way to get high.

By the 1970s, two out of three high school students had smoked marijuana at least once. Also in this period, the casualties of drug taking began to surface. Hospital emergency wards were treating more and more people who had taken hallucinogens and "freaked out" on "bad trips." Some had slipped into a temporary state of psychosis; a few had entered it permanently. Others had had car accidents or jumped off buildings while under the influence of various hallucinogens. Other drugs, such as amphetamines, or speed, were claiming casualties as well.

In 1970, *Time* magazine printed a feature article about the fall of America's most celebrated hippie community, the Haight-Ashbury neighborhood in San Francisco. The article described several murders that had occurred among this group and that involved people who were taking amphetamines. No one would ever forget the title of this feature story: "Speed Kills." From this point on, the idealistic "rap" about drugs—as consciousness enhancers or as spiritual aids—would live under the shadow of this negative press.

In the 1980s one other drug was introduced into the mainstream. Until that time, cocaine was used regularly only by a few very rich people, by people in the higher echelons of crime, or by those who also abused heroin. Most Americans thought that cocaine was dangerous and mysterious. It had not played a large role in the counterculture rebellion.

In the eighties cocaine became associated with a glamorous lifestyle and the fast profits that some people were able to accrue as a result of Reaganomics. Hollywood celebrities, Wall Street commodities brokers, and students at prestigious universities brought cocaine into the mainstream. Cocaine was expensive, but little was needed to feel the first few moments of high. In addition, very little research on the effects of long-term cocaine use existed. The drug became popular very quickly. Although media reports warned of the dangers of using this drug indiscriminately, none claimed that cocaine was addictive. There were no symptoms of physical withdrawal from the drug as there were from heroin, and few researches had followed its use over time. It took a stronger form of cocaine, known as crack, to reveal the addictive potentials of the drug. But by that time cocaine use was fully established in American culture.

In the nineties we are living with the legacy of the experiments that took place during the 1960s, 1970s, and 1980s. Cocaine, marijuana, and hashish have become part of the American scene. Almost no one defends these drugs anymore, yet a significant percentage of our population has tried them or uses them regularly.

The drug problem in America cannot be blamed totally on the counterculture of the sixties or the experiments with cocaine of the eighties. For drugs to become a real danger to this society, another element was needed: poverty.

It is no coincidence that drug abuse is often more prevalent in poor urban settings, where human misery prevails. When a doctor prescribes tranquilizers or mood elevators to someone suffering from nervous problems, an inability to sleep, or depression, these drugs are called medication. However, people who are numbing their bodies with heroin or alcohol or stimulating them with cocaine are also medicating themselves. They are doing it outside of any official medical contexts and without supervision, but they are probably medicating themselves for the same reason anyone would—to ease pain.

Many people who "self-medicate" with drugs live with the hopelessness and violence that go hand in hand with extreme poverty. Drugs may be their only "medicine" for the suffering caused by these problems. And self-medication can only increase when health care becomes too expensive or unavailable. Thus, after the drug experiments of the sixties and the extravagant cocaine escapades of the eighties, poverty is the next important player in the story of drugs in America. Poverty explains how cocaine—a drug once associated with Malibu Beach parties or Manhattan condominiums—took on the grim, violent, and desperate character it now exhibits among the nation's poor.

Drugs have been the subject of passionate debate since the 1960s. However, their effect upon small children was only lightly touched upon until the middle of the 1980s. The surgeon general warned that alcohol or cigarette smoking could cause birth defects, yet there was very little research on the effects of prenatal exposure to cocaine. There was a significant body of research on prenatal exposure to heroin and methadone, but the media did not publicize it. Then, in the mid-eighties, certain events brought the issue of parents, children, and drugs to the forefront of issues affecting our nation.

CHAPTER 2

DRUGS AND CHILDREN

TIME:	1986
PLACE:	New York City
NAME:	Judith Schaffer
OCCUPATION:	Adoption specialist

HER JOB was to try to increase the number of adoption placements in New York City. However, in 1986, Judith Schaffer began noticing an alarming trend. More and more child advocates were reporting bizarre behavior on the part of that year's babies. Many of the babies were strangely unresponsive or unmanageable. Foster parents complained that the children were more than they could handle.

Schaffer began reviewing the records of some of the problem babies. Every one of them had a mother who had used cocaine during pregnancy.[1] By 1988, Judith Schaffer was convinced beyond the shadow of a doubt that cocaine use during pregnancy could have devastating effects on the health and behavior of infants. She had spent two years preparing a report on the problem. Now she was ready to release it to the mayor's office.

After the release of the report, Schaffer was astonished to find that she was practically alone in her opinion that immediate action was necessary. The report was so frightening and the number of individuals involved was so high that the administration believed it would be bad policy to release it.

At the time, Schaffer had very little evidence beyond the experience of her own cases to back up her report. There were almost no studies linking cocaine use during pregnancy to birth defects or infant mortality. There was no consensus in the medical profession that cocaine could harm the developing fetus. Why, then, did the problem suddenly become apparent to this lone official in New York's vast welfare system? The answer is that 1986 marked the two-year anniversary of a new drug in New York City: crack.[2]

Crack is a smokeable form of cocaine. Cocaine, a derivative of the coca plant, is a stimulant that produces feelings of energy and euphoria. Once cocaine enters the bloodstream, it increases the brain's release of certain chemicals associated with pleasure. However, cocaine also overstimulates heartbeat and raises blood pressure to abnormal levels. When cocaine is sniffed in powder form, it takes several minutes to reach the brain and begin its effects, but when it is injected, it takes only ninety seconds. When cocaine is smoked in the form of crack, it reaches the brain in record time—only seven seconds.

Crack is similar to an older form of cocaine called freebase. Freebase cocaine is prepared though a complicated, flammable process of purification involving ether. This procedure is difficult and dangerous, but it produces a nearly pure form of the drug. When freebase is smoked, virtually all of the pure cocaine is delivered to the brain through the roof of the mouth and the lungs.

In 1984, a new, inexpensive form of freebasing called crack was developed. Preparation of crack requires only cocaine, baking soda, and water. This new form of cocaine hit the streets immediately. Before 1985, only the rich could afford it. But in that year crack cocaine, in the form of tiny white rocks that could be smoked in a glass pipe and cost as little as $3 to $5, came to New York City and other American urban centers.

Imagine a cheap, readily accessible form of cocaine

that reaches the brain in just seven seconds, boosting blood pressure in one burst, mercilessly pumping the heart, and exciting the user almost instantaneously. Such strong doses of cocaine as crack provides are extremely habit-forming. Since the cocaine is delivered to the brain and used up all at once, the user has to smoke every few minutes to keep up the high. Exactly how such a brutal chemical assault on the body of a pregnant woman can affect the developing fetus will be dealt with in the chapter on cocaine. For now it is important to know that it was crack that blew the whistle on how drugs can harm babies. Abnormalities were noticeable in a significant proportion of newborns who had been regularly exposed to crack in the womb. Although such reports were suppressed initially, statistics coming out of hospitals in New York, Chicago, Los Angeles, and other urban hospitals snowballed into a major health scandal by the end of 1988. In the end, there was no way to ignore what Judith Schaffer had pointed out.

The medical statistics concerned low birth weight, infant mortality, and birth defects. Of course, these problems had already existed to some extent for years. For two decades foundations like the March of Dimes had been developing research and community programs to deal with them. Infant mortality and low birth weight were already present in those same inner city neighborhoods where crack was about to strike. Professionals already knew that poor nutrition, a lack of prenatal care, and inadequate rest increased the chances of having an underweight child. So did habitual use of illegal drugs, drinking alcohol, or smoking while pregnant.

When crack hit the streets, it reversed the progress that had been made in dealing with low birth weight, infant mortality, and birth defects. The year 1986 had seen an all-time low of 12.4 infant deaths per 1,000 live births. By 1989, three short years later, the city's infant mortality rate had increased significantly. So had low birth weight, which is the single most significant determinant of infant mortality. Deaths were up 14 percent from what they had been in 1984.[3] This trend was typical not only of New York but of several other major American cities. The chart below shows how infant mortality changed across the nation in just two short years.

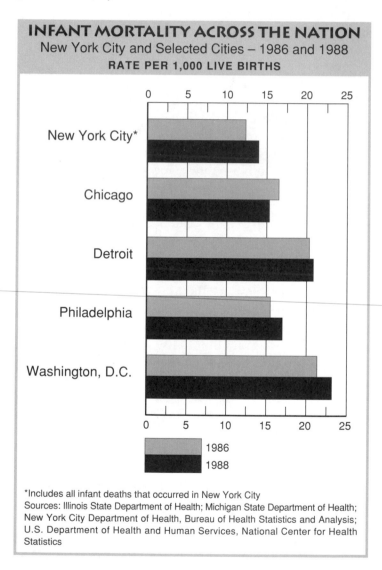

INFANT MORTALITY ACROSS THE NATION
New York City and Selected Cities – 1986 and 1988
RATE PER 1,000 LIVE BIRTHS

*Includes all infant deaths that occurred in New York City
Sources: Illinois State Department of Health; Michigan State Department of Health; New York City Department of Health, Bureau of Health Statistics and Analysis; U.S. Department of Health and Human Services, National Center for Health Statistics

In a booklet entitled "Infants at Risk," the Greater New York March of Dimes and the United Hospital Fund of New York stated in no uncertain terms what they assumed to be the primary cause of this depressing trend. "At least some of the deterioration can be attributed to the epidemic of substance abuse in the city," they warned. This assertion was backed up with some depressing statistics. In five years after the invasion of New York City by crack in 1984, more than 4,000 babies had been born to substance-abusing mothers. This represented an increase of 400 percent since 1980. Also by 1989, three out of four drug-exposed babies had been exposed to cocaine in one or more of its forms.[4] With other drug use remaining constant or increasing, the total number of drug-exposed babies being born in cities like New York had reached devastating proportions.

Until the mid-eighties, studies about babies exposed to drugs had dealt primarily with heroin, alcohol, and cigarette smoking. The media and the surgeon general had alerted the general public to the danger of smoking or drinking while pregnant. But it was crack that moved the issue of drugs and children to the forefront of the nation's consciousness. The years 1987 to the middle of 1991 saw a sudden flood of research, newspaper and magazine articles, TV reports, and large-scale studies of prenatal exposure to crack. Suddenly information was pouring in from every quarter.

Some of this information was based on solid scientific research. Other information came from the experiences of therapists, teachers, counselors, and other professionals working with the infants. Some information was autobiographical—the stories of foster parents who found themselves overwhelmed by the problems of trying to nurture crack-exposed babies. However, a good part of what was being presented as scientific fact was actually hysterical and exaggerated. Popular magazines spoke of a "lost generation" of damaged children who would never be able to

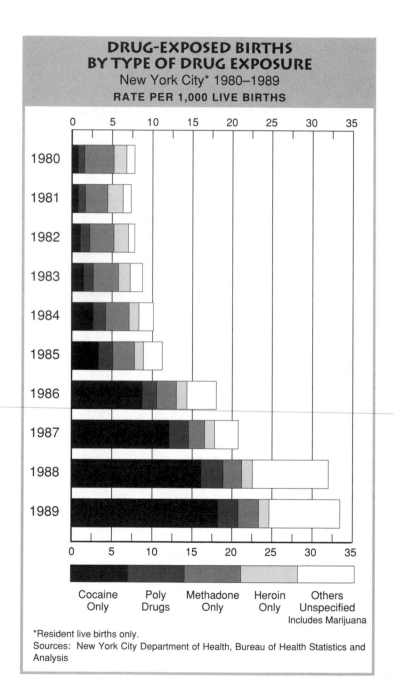

DRUG-EXPOSED BIRTHS
BY TYPE OF DRUG EXPOSURE
New York City* 1980–1989
RATE PER 1,000 LIVE BIRTHS

| | Cocaine Only | Poly Drugs | Methadone Only | Heroin Only | Others Unspecified Includes Marijuana |

*Resident live births only.
Sources: New York City Department of Health, Bureau of Health Statistics and Analysis

control their behavior, get an education, or hold a job. These years saw the forging of the new "crack baby" image. Mainstream magazines devoted feature articles to the chaotic world of "crack babies." They were portrayed as unresponsive to affection, unable to concentrate, irritable, and physically disabled.

Eventually the mis-information was sorted out, extremist views were rejected, and a new sophistication about the danger of drugs to children emerged. The solid statistics on drugs and children made people wonder how Judith Schaffer's report could ever have been ignored.

In 1994, no one doubted that prenatal exposure to drugs could cause serious problems. There is general agreement in the medical community that drug-exposed infants are at least four times more likely to be low birth weight and nearly three times more likely to die before their first birthday than nonexposed infants. The new awareness has caused heroin, methadone, and marijuana, as well as cocaine, to come under closer scrutiny.[5] Studies of combinations of drugs, such as methadone and cocaine, have shown that combining drugs may represent the gravest of dangers. Related studies are now examining what happens to babies when both mothers *and* fathers take drugs. Whereas a lack of concern about drugs and pregnancy ruled in many hospitals and in many offices of social services before, many professionals are now receiving special training to deal with the situation. Most now agree that the following rules apply when discussing prenatal exposure to drugs:

1. Low birth weight, infant mortality, and birth defects have all been linked directly to the use of alcohol and drugs.
2. Violence and child abuse are closely associated with the use of illegal drugs. Battered women are nine times as likely to abuse drugs.[6] The battering of women is often caused by the use of drugs itself. What is more,

25 percent to 40 percent of battered women were beaten while they were pregnant.

3. Drug-abusing fathers—not just mothers—have a serious effect upon infant health—both before conception, during pregnancy, and after the birth of the child. Many men also may influence their pregnant partners to use drugs.

4. Many other factors, including nutrition and prenatal care, determine how much harm drugs will do. Drug abuse during pregnancy cannot be studied without taking these other factors into account.[7]

5. One of the factors that determines how seriously a drug can damage an infant is how well it can penetrate the placenta. The placenta is the network of tissue and blood vessels that connects the mother's bloodstream to the fetus's. More scientific research regarding the abilities of various drugs to penetrate the placenta must be done.

6. A large part of the data about the likelihood, seriousness, and permanence of those symptoms seen shortly after birth is not in yet. No one yet knows how lasting some of the effects of drugs might be.

We have entered a new era of drug-abuse awareness. It is changing some of our oldest attitudes about pregnancy and child rearing. Education about drug abuse and pregnancy is rapidly spreading through the general population. In the future, few will ever be able to have a drink, light a cigarette, or take an illegal drug without being aware of the consequences. One only has to regret that it took a drug as devastating as crack cocaine to raise public awareness about the dangers of all drugs to children in general.

CHAPTER 3

COCAINE AND CRACK: THE EPIDEMIC AND ITS CONSEQUENCES

TIME:	1989
PLACE:	Hartford, Connecticut
NAME:	"Julia"
OCCUPATION:	Unemployed, susbstance abuser

IN JULY OF 1989, "Julia" injected cocaine just as she was about to go into labor. The child, a girl named Valerie, was born several hours later. She looked pale and was suffering from oxygen deprivation. Valerie was taken away from Julia by child welfare workers on the grounds that cocaine use before labor was a form of child abuse. However, lawyers for Julia intended to fight the decision. What the courts would decide depended partly upon how much hard proof there was that cocaine could really harm the fetus.

Julia's story appeared in *The New York Times*[1] because of the controversy about the accusations of child abuse. Could she really be charged with child abuse of a child that wasn't born yet? How much evidence was there to support the claim that cocaine use during pregnancy was a direct assault on the child? Studies have already shown that cocaine use can cause strokes, brain hemorrhages, blood vessel spasms, and other medical problems in adults. The challenge lay in proving that similar effects could be passed from mother to fetus.

Some readers of *The New York Times* must have been wondering why even an addicted woman would take cocaine so close to labor. There was no mention of her motives for injecting the drug in the article. But, believe it or not, many expectant mothers who use cocaine believe that using it close to the time of giving birth shortens the period of labor. In reality, it doesn't. The belief that it does has been disproved by a study at Hutzel Hospital in Detroit, Michigan.

What cocaine can do is cause the placenta to pull away from the wall of the uterus before labor. This pulling away of the placenta, known as *abruptio placentae*, usually causes a large flow of blood. The outcome can be fatal to both mother and baby. Many pregnant women who take cocaine may have a friend or acquaintance who has suffered from this very problem during labor. But this doesn't mean that they themselves will not smoke crack or take cocaine before they go to the hospital.

Even if cocaine use does not cause abruptio placentae during labor, there is a more than an average chance that labor will occur too early. Cocaine doesn't shorten the *period* of labor, but use of it late in pregnancy may make labor *begin* too early, before the fetus has reached full development.[2]

Cocaine is thought to be involved in a large proportion of prenatal drug problems today. From 1986 until the present time, crack caused a skyrocketing increase in the number of pregnant women taking drugs, while the number of pregnant women taking heroin and methadone stayed the same.[3] Cocaine use by women of childbearing age has increased more than 33 percent since 1985.[4] Although the percentage of women who are regular cocaine users is still less than that of men, female use has been increasing yearly.

Female cocaine use has taken a serious toll on the unborn and on infants of nursing age. At present, there are approximately 100,000 cocaine-exposed babies born each year in the United States. As early as the year 2000, the number of individuals exposed to cocaine before birth may reach 4 million.[5]

What are some of these cocaine-exposed babies like? How do those who end up taking responsibility for them deal with their problems? "Annie," a single woman from Brooklyn, New York, had been dreaming of adopting a healthy baby. In 1986 she let a social worker talk her into adopting six cocaine-exposed babies. Annie's chaotic life trying to raise these children was revealed in a 1990 *Rolling Stone* article.[6] Most likely because of their exposure to crack, her children experienced difficulty breathing, uncontrolled shaking, brain hemorrhages, seizures, and lung problems. Constant doctor's visits became a part of Annie's life. As if dealing with these health problems weren't enough, Annie's children also exhibited behavioral problems frequently associated with exposure to cocaine before birth. At times her daughter seemed incapable of playing the way other children do. She would pick up a block, throw it across the room at her brother, and then forget about it. Sometimes she seemed dazed. Her attention wandered from one toy to another or she forgot about playing altogether. One of Annie's sons could not seem to learn how to talk. Although Annie took him from specialist to specialist, no one could say for certain whether the symptom was connected to his mother's crack use and whether he would be able to learn to talk in the future.

Research on the effects of cocaine and crack on both adults and newborns is a relatively new field. No one can say for certain whether all the problems of Annie's children were caused by the cocaine their mothers took. However, numerous reports from hospitals, researchers, and parents confirm that at least some crack-exposed infants stiffen at one's touch, don't like to be held, and may flail and kick more than other newborns. Some do not walk or talk at the expected age or cannot learn to use

the toilet and dress themselves. Some are rowdy and disorganized, and others act so distant that they appear to be in a nearly catatonic state.[7]

The story of Annie's adopted children offers support for the theory that crack use can seriously harm the developing fetus, but it does not constitute scientific proof. No one knows for sure if cocaine was directly responsible for the children's abnormal behavior or physical problems. One can only infer it, because the mothers of these children took cocaine.

In the mideighties, a Chicago neonatologist named Ira Chasnoff began studying pregnant cocaine addicts in his clinic. His goal was to determine if there was a direct relationship between cocaine use and birth abnormalities. When the babies were born, he performed a series of tests on each. Chasnoff noticed right from the beginning that the circumferences of some of the babies' heads was smaller than normal. This is sometimes, but not always, a sign of mental retardation.[8] In the past, it has been associated with alcohol-exposed infants who were diagnosed as having certain mental abnormalities.

To find out if cocaine, like alcohol, could produce these abnormalities, researchers at the University of Texas Southwestern Medical Center in Dallas compared infants born to women who used cocaine, but not alcohol, during pregnancy to infants born to mothers who used neither alcohol nor cocaine and to infants whose mothers used alcohol but not cocaine.[9] The researchers concluded that brain growth of cocaine-exposed infants resembled that of alcohol-exposed infants. Both had an increased chance of being born with the same mental abnormalities.

Further studies by Chasnoff and others revealed other problems. Dr. Suzanne D. Dixon, a physician at the University of California at San Diego, found that a third of her study group of cocaine-exposed children had brain damage. Many similar studies with similar results have followed. However, to this date, no one has been able to prove a direct cause-and-effect relationship between cocaine use and any specific permanent defect. It is true that many children born to crack-using mothers are jittery and cry a lot during the first week of life, but this may be due to their withdrawal from cocaine. It may only be a passing phase.

Studies on cocaine's effect upon the human brain hint that the drug triggers the release of chemicals called endorphins. Endorphins are associated with emotional states of pleasure and well-being. As cocaine wears off, the release of endorphins diminishes. This change may be what makes "coming down" from cocaine or crack an unpleasant experience. It may be why some newborns exposed to crack go through a period of irritability and shakiness. No one has discovered exactly what happens to the brain after long-term, repeated doses of cocaine. Some researchers now believe that the "pleasure pathways" connecting nerve endings to endorphins begin to scar or wear out. In order to function properly, the brain may have to develop new pathways over time.[10] Whether infants who were exposed to crack through the placenta experience these long-term difficulties is still not known.

LOW BIRTH WEIGHT, INFANT MORTALITY, BIRTH DEFECTS AND COCAINE

The problem of low-birth weight babies was of serious concern for many years before the crack and cocaine crisis hit our nation's cities. A low-birth weight baby is one who weighs less than 5.5 pounds at birth. Low-birth weight babies often have to spend their first days, weeks, or even months in the hospital. They need special feeding procedures and medical treatments to be kept alive. The cost of medical care is substantial, and they are forty times more likely to die in their first month than normal-weight babies.

If they do survive, they will be at increased risk for such disabilities as mental retardation, cerebral palsy, or visual and hearing problems.[11]

Low birth weight is the single most important factor in infant mortality. Many low-birth weight babies die as a result of sudden infant death syndrome (SIDS). Sudden infant death syndrome is also known as "crib death." The syndrome sometimes occurs during sleep apnea, a condition in which the infant stops breathing for periods of time during sleep. With the advent of the cocaine crisis, researchers began wondering if there was a higher incidence of sudden infant death syndrome among infants who had been exposed to cocaine.

In Los Angeles County in 1986, a program was begun to link the medical histories of babies who had died of sudden infant death syndrome to their mother's cocaine and other substance abuse.[12] Researchers found a higher incidence of sudden infant death syndrome among infants who had been exposed to cocaine than among the general population. One cause of sudden infant death may be a condition known as respiratory distress syndrome. In infants with this condition, surfactant, a substance that coats the lung sacs, is missing. There is some evidence that cocaine may decrease surfactant, but further research is needed.

The degree of damage cocaine can cause in the fetus depends partly on the amount of cocaine able to reach the fetus through the mother's bloodstream. The highly veined tissue known as the placenta separates the mother's bloodstream from that of the fetus. All nourishment must pass in the form of fluids through this barrier of the placenta. Scientists know that some cocaine can penetrate the placental barrier—how much, however, is still a matter of conjecture.

The thesis that the cocaine that does reach the developing embryo can cause birth defects has been tested by a birth defect specialist named Ernest Zimmerman. At the

University of Cincinnati, Zimmerman injected pregnant mice with different doses of cocaine.[13] Shortly after the injection, the embryos were placed in artificial wombs. Within two days of development, blood began to pool in various parts of the embryos exposed to cocaine. Can such pooling lead to birth defects? Scientists now are studying the effects of pooling on the embryo.

Another important factor is the stage of prenatal development when the cocaine is taken. In the two weeks following fertilization, the egg seems invulnerable to most chemicals. But from the second to the eighth week, the embryonic organs of the fetus could be damaged. In fact, most dramatic deformities, such as missing limbs or cleft palates, are traced to this stage of development.

Scientists have known for a long time that a reduction in blood supply can cause damage to brain tissue.[14] Because cocaine use can reduce the supply of blood available to the fetus, large amounts of cocaine taken by a woman near the end of her pregnancy may cause the death of some tissues in the fetal brain. Brain damage that occurred in utero, due to a mother's cocaine use, may be the reason that some children who were exposed to crack or cocaine in the uterus are irritable. They cry more often and do not respond very favorably to human touch.

A researcher named Linda Spear and her colleagues at Binghamton University studied newborn rats that had been exposed to cocaine in the uterus. Baby rats have a preference for the odor of milk, which they associate with feeding time. The rats that had been exposed to cocaine did not associate the odor of milk with feeding. Spear interpreted this lack of association as a difficulty with learning. The same rats also showed an aversion to touch.

A higher incidence of seizures among cocaine-exposed babies has been reported. This indicates that cocaine may cause abnormalities of the nervous system. Many such neurological symptoms as seizures are examples of "soft" neurological damage.[15] "Soft" damage to the brain or nervous system cannot be measured easily. Data about it is collected mostly by observing how the babies act. Thus, it is difficult to establish conclusively the link between prenatal cocaine use and neurological symptoms.

"Soft" neurological data is not definitive proof of an actual birth defect, but it does give medical professionals cause for concern. Infants who were exposed to cocaine sometimes perform poorly on responsiveness tests. When they are as old as one month, some still perform under the level of responsiveness of two-day-olds. Cocaine-exposed babies also tend to be easily overstimulated.[16] The hugging, caressing, and cooing that most babies love cause some cocaine-exposed babies to arch their backs, cry in a high, catlike wail, and flap their arms. Such a cry, which has been dubbed a "crack cry," could be a sign of neurological damage.[17] Other cocaine-exposed babies react in a different way when they are overstimulated. They avoid the stimulus by slipping into a deep, day-long sleep.[18]

At the University of California at San Diego, researchers investigated whether some babies who had been exposed to crack and exhibited these "soft" behavioral symptoms also had physical abnormalities. In the eighty-two babies they examined, about a third had lesions in the brain, primarily in the areas that control thinking and learning. Whether such lesions will heal or will have long-term effects is still not known, since the brain continues to develop during the first year of life.[19]

Unfortunately, neurological problems are only part of the picture. One may associate strokes and other heart problems with old age, but some cocaine-exposed babies apparently may have such problems from the moment they take their first breath. For some time, hospitals have been reporting cocaine-exposed babies with malformed hearts, abnormalities on electrocardiograph tests, or evidence of strokes. Finding out whether cocaine use alone is responsible for these problems has been difficult for researchers. However, one study in January 1991 at a Boston hospital found data strongly suggesting that cocaine is directly related to strokes and other circulatory disorders.[20]

It is difficult to link cocaine use to birth defects because of the problems of studying human subjects while they are pregnant. Researchers must find a way not to disrupt pregnancies or endanger the fetus. Often researchers have to rely upon a mother's word as to whether or not she is an abuser of cocaine. Urine screens taken at the time of delivery can detect cocaine use during the previous few days but can tell nothing about earlier cocaine use.[21] About 50 percent of cocaine users are missed by urine tests.[22] What is more, it is hard to differentiate between cocaine and other illicit drugs used during pregnancy. Many cocaine users also smoke, drink, and take other drugs. They often have diets poor in nutrition and receive no prenatal care. All of these can be factors in the infant deaths, birth defects, and abnormal behavior of cocaine-exposed babies.

As recently as April 1992, researchers at Emory University in Atlanta still claimed that "the extent to which cocaine has specific effects distinct from those associated with polydrug use and the lifestyle common among addicted and substance-using women remains unclear."[23] Several researchers are now analyzing the chemical compounds produced by the body when it processes cocaine and another drug at the same time. The results of this research may determine the degree to which such combinations harm the fetus.

OTHER FACTORS

The dangers to children from maternal cocaine use can continue for months and even years after birth. Cocaine remains in the user's bloodstream for a long period of time. Preliminary research indicates that it may enter the mother's milk and be imparted to the infant during breast-feeding. A recent study of female rats exposed to cocaine found that the amount of cocaine in their milk was eight times as much as that in their blood.[24] If this is true in the case of humans, the children of cocaine-abusing mothers would be getting doses of cocaine in the very milk that feeds them. One would expect these babies to suffer from the same problems as adults who ingest cocaine: nervous system abnormalities, increased heartbeat, elevated blood pressure, and eventual addiction.

Even children who are not breast-fed may be getting regular doses of the drug from cocaine-using mothers. In the February 26, 1992, issue of the *Journal of the American Medical Association*, a writer speculated that secondhand crack smoke was a danger to children in households where the drug was being smoked. The article was based on reports from the emergency room at Children's Hospital of Michigan in Detroit, where cocaine by-products had been found in the urine of more than 5 percent of the children being treated there. In order to come to even tentative conclusions about the danger of secondhand crack smoke, researchers had to rule out other possible routes of exposure, such as previous in utero exposure, breast milk, or actual application of cocaine to parts of the child's body. Though the study was far from conclusive, it did suggest that breathing secondhand crack smoke could be comparable to actually taking the drug.

Another danger to children whose parents take cocaine is a lack of prenatal care. Inadequate prenatal care diminishes the chances of a child's being born healthy. In a 1991 study of inner city women, infants of women with minimal or no prenatal care had a lower mean birth weight and a higher frequency of prematurity.[25] Women who neglected to seek prenatal care were also more likely to be single, smoke cigarettes, and abuse drugs—especially cocaine.

As you remember from chapter 1, intoxicants are substances that alter thought patterns and emotions and thus affect behavior. Women and men who take cocaine are revving up their senses to high levels of excitation. Some users claim that the drug seems to make anything they normally like to do "even better." Thus, good conversationalists are likely to get into nonstop talking jags when they take cocaine. People who like to dance might find themselves caught in a dance marathon, in which the excitement of movement and rhythm sweeps them away. In fact, almost any activity that seems pleasurable in a normal state may be enhanced. That is why cocaine sometimes acts as an aphrodisiac. Nights of insatiable sex have been reported by cocaine users who were carried away by pleasure signals being fired with abnormal frequency in their brains.

Pleasure signals in the brain aren't the only reason for increased sexual activity among some cocaine users. Another reason is cocaine's unbearable "down." As the drug wears off, the sense of emptiness and physical discomfort can be unbearable. Many users resort to sexual stimulation to take their mind off "coming down."[26] A loss of sexual inhibitions and increased sexual activity may be reasons for the correlation between cocaine use and positive tests for HIV and syphilis.[27]

If a woman who is positive for AIDS conceives a child, there is a 25 percent to 35 percent chance that the child will become infected in the womb as the virus passes through the placenta.[28] If an infected male partner carries the virus, he may pass it on to the woman during intercourse, and she in turn may pass it on to the fetus. Syphilis infections that develop during pregnancy can also be extremely dangerous. They may cause birth defects such as poor eyesight, mental retardation, or deformed bones.[29]

Another big risk of crack and cocaine use is that it often occurs in an atmosphere of violence. A 1993 Public Health Report[30] stated that one-fifth to one-third of all women are physically abused during their lifetime, often by a current or former partner. The report recognized a "trigger effect" between alcohol and drug abuse and domestic violence. In many cases, abuse occurs while a woman is pregnant. When blows and kicks are directed toward the abdomen, both mother and fetus may suffer irreparable damage. In other cases, abuse begins with a mother and then spills over into abuse of the child, while the battered mother stands by, helplessly begging the abuser to stop hurting the baby.

Of course, a mother herself can be responsible for the abuse of an infant. The evening news in most large cities has no lack of stories about cocaine-using mothers who maimed or even killed children while they were high or coming down. The black depressions suffered by cocaine addicts threaten a child's general safety, mood, and ability to learn.

Addicted mothers run a greater than average risk of having negative feelings about pregnancy and parenting.[31] Imagine adding to this a cocaine-exposed baby's tendency to cry constantly and resist being held. The combination of factors makes it difficult for mother and child to bond. Bonding between mother and child through deep feelings of attachment and love is essential to the healthy development of a child. But bonding can be difficult or impossible for some cocaine-exposed babies. A percentage of the babies seem unable to distinguish between their mother and strangers.

CHAPTER 4

OPIATES:
THE BABY ADDICTS

TIME:	1980
PLACE:	New York City
NAME:	Crystal Taylor
OCCUPATION:	Student

ONE NIGHT Crystal, age ten, was in her room when she heard her mother screaming. She ran into the kitchen and discovered that her father was foaming at the mouth. His eyes were turned upward so that only the whites were showing. The kitchen table was strewn with needles and bloody tissues. Crystal's mother was frantically trying to stuff ice down her father's throat. Crystal thought her father was dead and ran to tell a neighbor. The ambulance arrived in time to save him from a heroin overdose this particular time. The next night, Crystal walked into the kitchen to discover her mother injecting the heroin that had been left over.[1]

Until the eighties, heroin, not cocaine, was the drug that represented the greatest danger to adults and children. Heroin is an opiate, a derivative of the poppy plant *Papaver somniferum*, also known as the opium poppy. All opiates depress the nervous system and suppress sensitivity to pain. One opium derivative still used today in hospitals is morphine. It is injected into the bodies of individuals who are suffering from extreme pain. Morphine is one of the strongest painkillers medically available, but it must be administered with extreme caution. Tolerance to morphine and other opiates develops quickly. People who use them too long require increasingly stronger and stronger doses to achieve the same relief.

Opiates are physically addictive. When they are withdrawn from someone who has developed a tolerance for them, that person becomes extremely ill. Symptoms include nausea, trembling, diarrhea, severe cramps, crawling skin and goose bumps, vomiting, runny nose, tearing eyes, and sometimes convulsions. To avoid these unbearable symptoms, many users will do almost anything to get more of the drug. In extreme cases, their craving for the drug can overcome all their moral scruples. Accordingly, Crystal Taylor's mother probably went right back to taking the heroin that had almost killed Crystal's father because she felt she had no choice. Her gnawing hunger for the drug overcame her concern for her own young and impressionable child who had just witnessed her father almost being killed by the drug. For those addicted to heroin, avoiding the sickness of withdrawal can become more important than any other life event.

Heroin, a powerful derivative of morphine, was first developed in Germany in 1898. Later, hospitals abandoned the use of heroin as a painkiller because it was too addictive and side effects were uncontrollable. But this did not happen until illicit use of the drug had grown to alarming proportions.

If you are a city dweller, you may be familiar with some of the mannerisms, lifestyles, and problems associated with heroin use. The typical heroin user's stance on the street is a bent-knee weaving. The user will "nod" in and out of consciousness, and will have difficulty maintaining balance. Thus, a person on heroin trying to cross the street may "nod out" in the middle of traffic, sway on bent knees as if about to fall, then suddenly regain full consciousness, realize that he or she is in the middle of the street, and continue walking.

Heroin can be sniffed, injected, or smoked. Until recently, most longtime users injected it intravenously—in other words, directly into the veins. Various problems arose from this. A longtime heroin user may need a fresh shot as frequently as five or six times a day. Eventually the veins collapse from being continually punctured. In the search for new veins, the user may try any available surface of the body, including the forearms, backs of the hands, wrists, legs, between the toes, in the neck, armpit, or genitals. Thus, habitual users are often recognizable by the scars, needle marks, and patterns of collapsed veins (called "tracks") all over their body.

Intravenous injection of heroin is rarely, if ever, done under sterile conditions. Even an addict who does not share needles with other users probably uses the same needle many times without cleaning it adequately. What is more, street heroin is almost always cut with other substances. Thus, each time a person "shoots up," he or she is injecting many contaminants into the veins. Bacteria that cling to the needle sometimes cause blood infections that require strong antibiotic treatment. Needles can also spread the hepatitis B virus, which can seriously damage the liver. The substances used to cut heroin, such as baby laxative and talc, can also strain the liver, which must act to filter them. If the impurities are toxic enough, they may even cause death.

Since the early 1980s, the most serious risk from injecting heroin has been the contraction of the HIV virus. Addicts have always shared needles—both for practical purposes and for the communal feeling of shooting up together. If one of the addicts using a needle is carrying the HIV virus, the virus may survive in a drop of blood left inside the hollow shaft of a needle. The HIV virus does not survive long when it is exposed to air. But the hollow chamber of a hypodermic needle can keep it away from oxygen long enough to allow it to infect the addict who next uses the needle. The 1980s saw an epidemic of AIDS among intravenous drug users. To avoid the risk of contracting AIDS, some users now sniff heroin or smoke it instead of injecting it. Others, who have been educated by community outreach programs, refuse to share needles without first cleaning them with bleach. But many new cases of HIV infections through infected needles are still being reported.

Like the father of Crystal Taylor, heroin users also constantly risk overdosing. Because street heroin is never pure, an addict can never be sure about the strength of an injection. A "bag" from one batch of heroin may barely produce a high in a seasoned user. But a second bag the same size may be purer and may contain more heroin. Shooting this "good" bag can lead to an overdose that stops respiration and heartbeat and kills the user.

To make matters worse, in the late 1980s, a new "designer drug" made from fentanyl hit the streets of the East Coast. It was not expensive to make and was hundreds of times as powerful as pure heroin. Fentanyl is sometimes used in extremely small, controlled amounts to lower respiration during surgery. One grain the size of a grain of salt crushed into a bag of street heroin with other fillers may be enough to get an addict high. Just two grains could kill someone. This is what happened in the late eighties and early nineties when fentanyl was snuck into bags of heroin sold under such enticing names as Tango and Cash, Tombstone, and D.O.D. (Dead on Delivery). Word got around that this was happening, but, unbelievably, the news attracted more users in search of stronger highs. Hundreds of deaths occurred as a result.

Heroin users are typically undernourished and unwashed. All their money goes to the drug because its cost can be astronomical. While a ten-dollar bag may satisfy some for a day, others need six, ten, or even twenty times that amount just to keep from experiencing withdrawal symptoms. They have little money left for food or lodging, and some become homeless. Being high in the street also makes them prone to falls, assaults from others, and exposure to cold. However, some addicts pay little mind to their deteriorating conditions as long as they are able to stay high.

In the 1960s and 1970s urban governments became increasingly concerned about heroin use. The culture that grew up around large clusters of users in poor areas threatened the safety of the streets. To avoid withdrawal, addicts sometimes went to gruesome extremes. They would beg for money, steal purses, rob their own children, or housebreak. Concern for a relative or friend evaporated in the discomfort of withdrawal. An epidemic of crime and violence flourished around the context of heroin as people who were "hooked" on the drug sought bolder and bolder solutions to keep up the flow of money needed to maintain the habit. A controversy about the best way to deal with the problem raged in the public health field, law enforcement agencies, and state and city governments. Some cited a recent program for addicts in England that offered free, dose-controlled heroin regularly to any documented addict who signed up. The rate of crime among these addicts was much lower than it was among American heroin users, because the English addicts did not have to steal to get the drug. In America, however, heroin remained illegal even for medical purposes. Some local governments had to resort to another drug that was not illegal in all contexts: methadone.

Although methadone too is highly addictive, when taken regularly by a heroin user, it suppresses withdrawal symptoms. In the United States, methadone maintenance programs became the primary answer to the urban heroin crisis. The drug has many unpleasant side effects: gastrointestinal problems, sleepiness or jitteriness, and long-term destruction of some organs. But it was thought that it would save users from withdrawal pains and at least lower the incidence of drug-associated crimes.

Methadone programs have since been revealed as fraught with problems. These programs do lower the risk of contracting AIDS, overdosing, or polluting the body with the impurities of street heroin. However, methadone maintenance programs assume a sense of responsibility and timing on the part of some addicts that just does not exist. Those who miss their daily dose of methadone because they oversleep or forget to show up are abruptly thrown back into old habits. They end up buying methadone from the black market that flourishes outside of some clinics or they go back to heroin. Also, some people mix methadone with other drugs, such as tranquilizers, barbiturates, or alcohol to accentuate the effects of the drug. Finally, long-term use of methadone can cause health problems that are not yet completely understood. And methadone administered to pregnant women is suspected of affecting the developing fetus. Nevertheless, methadone may have done some good. Perhaps because of it, the number of people on opiates in this country has remained fairly constant for the last ten years, whereas the use of cocaine and crack has escalated.

The effect of heroin and methadone on the body and on the lifestyles of their users is distressing enough, but we must also consider what happens when heroin is used in a family context. For some addicts the demands of parenting are added to the unhealthy bodies, psychological stress, poverty, crime, and desperate living that are part of the heroin lifestyle. Needless to say, the heroin-addicted lifestyle is in no way suitable for the raising of healthy children.

The story of Crystal Taylor's father overdosing could be considered mild in comparison to what has happened to some children whose parents take heroin. These children never know when they may wake up to find the television or their tricycle lost to a "strung-out" father or mother who combs the streets at dawn, hoping to sell these possessions for a bag. A child may witness a violent fight among parents for the last shot that remains. Parents who are high all the time may neglect to feed their children or to buy them clothes. During episodes of withdrawal, the child may be the one who suffers from the violence of a parent's frustration. Heroin-ravaged families may find themselves homeless or without food. Or the parent may become ill from hepatitis or AIDS or die from an overdose. Of course, there is also a chance that the child may have contracted the HIV virus before being born. Whether or not all or some of these problems occur, there is a strong possibility that the child will spend some time in foster homes.

Such tragedies are common knowledge among social service workers. However, only in the 1970s were investigations begun into the damage that heroin can cause the fetus. This is appalling, because one connection between heroin and pregnancy has been recognized for over forty years: the babies of heroin-using mothers are often themselves born addicted to heroin.[2] The first hours of life are spent in the agony of withdrawing from the drug.

Heroin-addicted babies have been shown to suffer from a variety of physical problems. However, no one is absolutely sure whether these problems are caused by heroin damage to the fetus during pregnancy or merely by the stress of withdrawing from heroin shortly after birth. Opiate drugs are distributed to the fetus across the placenta,[3] and heroin-exposed babies have a higher incidence of infant deaths, low birth weight, and failure to thrive. However, researchers just don't know when and how damage to these babies occurs. They also don't know which of the abnormalities will persist into adulthood.

One very noticeable phenomenon in children born to heroin-addicted mothers is their abnormal sleep patterns. Sleep researchers describe two types of human sleep, which most of us experience nightly. The deeper of the two kinds of sleep is quiet sleep (QS). It is characterized by a minimum of movement and deep, slow, restful breathing. The second kind of sleep is rapid-eye-movement sleep (REMS). Researchers have discovered that dreaming occurs during the period of REM sleep. The eyes move rapidly back and forth under the eyelids as if following the dream scenario. Heroin-exposed babies show a decrease in quiet sleep and an increase in REM when compared to normal children. Consequently, they are not getting as profound a rest as they need. Heroin-exposed babies are also more likely to be hyperactive and have less-developed motor skills.[4]

Whether these persistent symptoms can be blamed on the stress of the withdrawal period shortly after birth or on previous damage to the nervous system still remains to be shown. In the studies of the effects of heroin abuse upon the health of the fetus, researchers have run up against the same problems as in their studies of cocaine exposure. Because they fear damaging human fetuses, researchers must study animal subjects, such as the fetal lamb. Animal experience with drugs in some ways closely parallels human experience, but in other ways it differs significantly.

Pregnant women's participation in methadone programs has given researchers a chance to study addicts both during pregnancy and after the child is born. However, these studies can only suggest what the results with heroin would be. Most of the women in the methadone program have stopped taking heroin. Although methadone use has similar effects on the body, the two drugs are far from identical.

All studies of pregnant women who take only heroin

have been fraught with uncertainties. It is next to impossible to isolate heroin use, because many of these women also use other drugs, drink alcohol, smoke, and have other experiences stressful to their health. What is more, it is impossible to know what substances the heroin is being cut with or which microorganisms are being transmitted to the body by dirty needles. Also, addicts rarely come in for regular prenatal checkups. Many fear that their child will be taken away from them if it is discovered that they are addicts. Others lack the funds for medical care or the transportation to reach it. Some are fed up with the insensitive, judgmental remarks of certain poorly trained health care workers they have encountered. Their missed medical visits prevent frequent screening of their urine for opiates. To make matters worse, habitual heroin users often have unreliable long-term memories. This makes the taking of case histories next to impossible.[5]

As with crack and cocaine, detecting heroin use is a real challenge to researchers because the substance is illegal. Its use always occurs in situations where there are no guidelines, no control, and no record keeping. Researchers have the difficult task of studying behavior that occurs in an underground, lawless context.

Several recent studies have sought to lay some new groundwork in the study of prenatal exposure to heroin. Babies were selected for study who required treatment at birth for withdrawal symptoms and who were restless, had sleep problems, and had tantrums during the first year of life.[6] At least a fifth of such children seem to continue to have problems for several years afterward.[7] Some researchers think these problems are due to lasting physical abnormalities caused by exposure to heroin. But others wonder how many of these problems come from the social settings of heroin use. Even if the bodies of babies born to heroin-using mothers are physically normal, continued exposure to violence, unreliable parents, poor nutrition, and other problems frequently associated with the drug lifestyle might cause long-standing problems.

The researchers compared heroin-exposed children to normal children and to children whose mothers were on methadone maintenance. It was thought that the methadone groups would reveal something about the effects of the lifestyle of the heroin user. Methadone and heroin have similar chemistries, yet mothers on methadone are more likely to get regular medical checkups. They do not suffer as many episodes of painful withdrawal; nor do they have to put themselves in violent situations to get their medication.

The researchers concluded that heroin intake by a pregnant woman might have some small permanent neurological effect upon the child, including minor problems with motor coordination and a difficulty in concentrating. However, it does not appear to cause major long-term disabilities or behavior problems in children.[8] The more likely cause of these problems is the social atmosphere of heroin addiction.

The life of a heroin-exposed child may be difficult at first, and the effects of this pain may extend for several months or even years into life. But neither in utero exposure to heroin nor the withdrawal process after birth are permanent handicaps to the developing child.

In the 1980s, researchers at Cornell University Medical College sought a closer view of the action of opiates on the fetal nervous system. They already had extensive data for comparison, but all of it involved tests performed on adult humans and adult animals under the influence of opiates. There was no way to perform tests on an unborn fetus exposed to heroin without harming the fetus or interfering with its growth. The researchers would have to study fetal lambs instead of humans, keeping in mind that what was true for animals might not always be true for humans.[9]

In the course of their study, the researchers established an interesting characteristic of opiates. Many scientists had focused on their action as depressants, which slow down all body systems. The new research showed that although this was true for some doses, different amounts of the drugs could either depress or *speed up* breathing.

The researchers' results confirmed what addicts on the streets had known for years. Addicts have always reported that their "nods" are sometimes interrupted by sudden surges of restlessness. Their head jerks up and their body seems charged with nervous energy. At such a moment they might scratch themselves maniacally, tremble in the limbs and feet, or begin to chatter, only to have this flutter of activity cut off by another deep nod.[10]

If the effects of opiates on fetuses are similar, one could expect the fetus to fall in and out of deep, comalike states alternating with sudden moments of restless energy and rapid breathing. And indeed, the REM-charged sleep of babies born to addicts is suggestive of this frenetic restlessness within a depressed comalike state. However, how such abrupt changes in energy levels may be harming fetuses' brains, organs, and personalities remains to be discovered.

The same researchers also wanted to know what happens to the cardiovascular output of the fetus when the mother takes heroin or other opiates. Traditionally, opiates were thought to slow heartbeat and lower blood pressure in adults. But more-recent studies have revealed tachycardia, or an abnormally rapid heartbeat, in some people under the influence of opiates at certain times. Researchers soon found the same tachycardia in lamb fetuses exposed to opiates; but strangely, the drug *never* produced slowed heartbeats in these fetuses at any doses and at any time. The fact that opiates seem to affect fetuses somewhat differently than they do adults raises many questions for further research.

In Sweden, researchers made a bold attempt to evaluate some of the possible hidden long-term effects of opiate use on the unborn. At the Ulleraker University Hospital in Uppsala, they compared the histories of opiate addicts born between 1945 and 1965 with those of their nonaddicted brothers and sisters born during the same period. They determined that a large percentage of those who had become opiate addicts had mothers who had been given opiates or certain other drugs within ten hours before delivery. Some of the mothers had been given the opiates only once.

The authors of the study have suggested a curious explanation for this finding. They theorize that human newborns can be "imprinted" during the early moments of life. The classic definition of imprinting concerns studies of baby geese who follow the first stimulus they see shortly after being hatched. If they see their mother, they will follow her, but if they see another stimulus, ranging from an inflated balloon to an adult human, they will follow it as if it were their mother. The Swedish theorists have suggested that perhaps the opiate "imprinted" itself upon the infants shortly before birth. This imprinting created a lifetime attachment to the opium "high," which caused these individuals to become addicts later.[11] If this is true, using opiates even at the very end of pregnancy may be sealing a child's future. Even if the mother was merely "experimenting" and does not become addicted, her behavior may raise the ante for a life of drug addiction in the next generation.

Despite the problems of heroin-addicted women and their children, these mothers are today considered less handicapped for child raising than crack-addicted mothers. Michelle Rogers, a woman from Brooklyn, is one example of a woman who nearly lost her entire family to heroin but has since taken control of her life.[12] In 1989 she was summoned to court, and her children were placed in foster care. The court decision came as the result of a long decline during which she had struggled with heroin addiction and a lack of housing. She had started using drugs in 1985, after the breakup of her marriage, when she and her children were placed in a hotel for homeless families, not far from the city airport. The hotel was a crack-infested and violent place. While mothers, fathers, and boyfriends got high, children, unwashed, unfed, and unsupervised, played in the hallways.

Michelle Rogers says she fell into heroin addiction because it was the only temporary relief from what seemed like a bottomless depression. "I was medicating myself with heroin so that I could get through the day," she told a *New York Times* reporter who interviewed her at the courthouse. Although she gradually became addicted to the drug, she never injected it. And she was careful never to let her kids see her get high.

By 1991, Michelle Rogers had pulled her life together through an outpatient drug program and was searching for housing. She came back to court and petitioned to regain custody of her children. The judge was sympathetic. The judge's experience with addicts and recovered addicts suggested that mothers with a history of heroin abuse were more able to put their lives back together than those who had used crack. On the strength of this assumption and on the progress Michelle Rogers had made, the judge ordered that her children be returned to her as soon as she was able to find housing.

Would the judge's remarks about heroin-using mothers have been so optimistic fifteen or twenty years ago? At that time the drug provided the most devastating examples of how drugs can ruin lives and families. But now, with the majority of neglect cases tied to crack, Michelle Rogers' heroin-sniffing problem seems, to take on a more benign cast. The fact that she is no longer addicted and is actively seeking to get her children back offers some proof that children can be reclaimed by their recovered parents.

Current research suggests that prenatal exposure to heroin has few serious long-term effects. If the violent, neglectful atmosphere of heroin can be eliminated from the growing child's environment, then the baby born heroin-addicted may stand a chance for a healthy, normal future.

CHAPTER 5

ALCOHOL: THE BRAIN-CELL DESTROYER

TIME:	1968
PLACE:	Paris, France
NAME:	Paul Lemoine
OCCUPATION:	Pediatrician

TODAY all alcoholic beverages sold in the United States contain a warning to pregnant women, and all restaurants and bars that serve alcohol are required to post the following message:

> *According to the surgeon general, women should not drink alcoholic beverages during pregnancy because of the risk of birth defects.*

Despite the new awareness of the harmful effects of alcohol on the developing fetus, over 50,000 babies are born each year with birth defects associated with alcohol.[1] The statistic is alarming in the face of recent efforts to educate women on the danger of drinking while pregnant, but it is also understandable. Alcoholism is a disease that is not always corrected by education. An alcoholic may be very aware of the dangers of drinking but find it impossible to stop. According to a recent Epidemiologic Catchment Area Study by the National Institute of Mental Health, 3 percent of all women of childbearing age abuse alcohol or are alcoholics. Yet only a fraction of these women will ever receive treatment for the disease.

In the 1950s, when this writer was born, some pediatricians would suggest that breast-feeding mothers drink a beer or two a day. No one seemed to consider that the alcohol in the beer might find its way into the breast milk or have some effect on the milk's chemical structure.

It was not until 1968, in France, that alcohol began to receive closer scrutiny in the context of pregnancy, breast-feeding, and child raising. A French pediatrician, Paul Lemoine, had begun noticing facial deformities in the infants of mothers who drank heavily.[2] All of them had small heads, flattened noses under a jutting brow, a thin upper lip, and malformed ears.

Lemoine's findings at first didn't arouse much interest in France, where the economy depends partly on the sale of wine. Besides, many alcoholic mothers gave birth to children who appeared completely normal. Further studies, however, established that these symptoms were only the tip of the iceberg. Researchers were soon to discover that alcohol can seriously damage the fetal brain, producing a set of conditions called *fetal alcohol effects*. Symptoms range from mental retardation to slowed growth and behavioral problems. The more severe effects of alcohol use during pregnancy are known as *fetal alcohol syndrome*. To be diagnosed with this syndrome, a person must exhibit the following three major symptoms:

1. slowed growth, before birth and/or after birth
2. facial abnormalities, including small head, small eye slits, crossed eyes, a flattened midface, and a thin upper lip
3. problems of the central nervous system, including learning and development problems, hyperactivity, trouble paying attention, and mental retardation.[3]

Fetal alcohol syndrome, one of the most common causes of mental retardation in this country, occurs in about one in 3,000 births. It can harm not only the nervous system but virtually every other body system. Prenatal exposure to alcohol has been known to cause heart and circulatory problems, kidney problems, skeletal problems, and muscular problems.[4] Not every woman who drinks heavily will have a child with full-blown fetal alcohol syndrome. The percentage of children of alcoholic women who have the syndrome is actually quite low—about 6 percent.[5] However, the less serious fetal alcohol effects are harder to measure, and there aren't as many statistics on them.

As with other substances, researchers' only means of observing the action of alcohol on fetuses is by observing the fetuses of animals. Recent experiments with animals have revealed some of the chemical reactions that occur inside the body of the mother and inside the developing fetus. Researchers especially value these animal experiments because they allow them to control for other forms of drug abuse, for smoking, and for poor nutrition. The role of smoking in cases of fetal alcohol syndrome is extremely important. Researchers have noticed that even moderately alcoholic mothers may produce children with fetal alcohol syndrome if they are also heavy smokers.[6] However, researchers cannot always be certain that the animals they are studying react in the same way to alcohol as human subjects do. In working with animals, they have to investigate these differences and correct for them as best they can.

In 1992, at the State University of New York at Albany, researchers fed newborn rat pups milk spiked with alcohol for only two days. Although the rats were already born, their brain development was in many ways equal to that of human fetuses in their last three months of development. In the brains of the alcohol-fed pups, the protein that protects brain cells was being produced at higher than normal levels. Protective protein is produced in the human brain when its cells are injured. Why was there so much of it being produced by the alcohol-fed rats? The researchers took this as a sign that the alcohol had turned on a stress signal in the rats' brains because cells were being damaged.[7]

Researchers who study only humans cannot very easily observe alcohol in the act of damaging brain cells or other body systems. They have to be satisfied with "after-the-fact" diagnoses and long-term studies of people exposed to alcohol before birth. In general, their research can take three approaches: studying people who have been diagnosed as having fetal alcohol syndrome, studying all children of known alcoholic mothers, and studying children who were exposed before birth to any level of alcohol at all.[8] In studying these three groups researchers have tried to establish some kind of standard of risk. In other words, how much does a mother have to drink in order to endanger her fetus? Also, in what period of pregnancy is drinking most dangerous?

These questions have been far from easy to answer. Too many other factors are involved. Damage to the fetus seems to depend as much on the timing of the doses as on the total amount that the mother drinks. The development of fetal alcohol syndrome in the child may be also determined by the mother's health, her socioeconomic class, and her lifestyle. Also, once a woman has a child with fetal alcohol syndrome, the chances of her having another is as high as 70 percent, even if she has stopped drinking.[9] This suggests that alcohol may cause permanent damage to a woman's reproductive system.[10]

Even before fetal alcohol syndrome was defined, it was common knowledge among medical professionals that people who drink a great deal are often malnourished. Alcohol provides carbohydrate calories that yield high energy, so a drink can resemble a meal. But people who drink their meals are not getting vitamins, minerals, or protein.[11] Long before studies on substance abuse and pregnancy, it was noticed that malnourished mothers often did not produce healthy babies. As a matter of fact, fetal alcohol syndrome might itself be caused by something as simple as malnourishment. Some mothers who drink a lot have vitamin or protein deficiencies. Alcohol also inhibits the production of one component of vitamin A, called retinoic acid. Some researchers now believe that a lack of retinoic acid may be the major reason for the birth defects associated with fetal alcohol syndrome.[12]

You may remember from the chapter on cocaine that there are periods of pregnancy when harm to the fetus through cocaine use is more likely. Some of the same rules hold in alcohol abuse. Exposure to a harmful substance from the second to the eighth week, when organs are developing, can result in major birth defects. But growth of the fetus can be affected at any time. The brain is vulnerable to damage at various times as well, because the brain is constantly developing throughout the pregnancy.[13]

In interviewing many women about their drinking patterns during pregnancy, researchers became aware of one important factor. Because women often do not know they are pregnant until several weeks after conception, they can unwittingly expose the fetus to alcohol very early in the pregnancy. One large-scale study found that women who drank during the first two months of pregnancy ran an increased risk of having low-birth weight babies, babies with small heads, and babies less than the normal length. These babies were also more at risk for mental retardation.[14] The fact that women cannot always identify the exact time of conception has confused some studies comparing those who drink at the beginning of pregnancy with those who do not drink at all during pregnancy.

How much does a women have to drink while pregnant to put her baby at serious risk? It is believed today that any pregnant woman who drinks more than 3 ounces of alcohol (six drinks) a day is running the risk of having a baby with fetal alcohol syndrome or at least some of the serious fetal alcohol effects.[15] Lesser amounts—as low as three drinks per day—have been associated with children who score lower than the normal level on IQ tests by the age of four. Even two drinks per day have been shown to cause reduced birth weight and neurological abnormalities.[16] At the present time the rule of thumb is this: Nobody knows for certain how much is safe to drink during pregnancy. Too many factors play a part in the final outcome. So pregnant women who are concerned about not harming their baby are advised not to drink at all.

Recently, new research has added to the list of problems that may be caused by drinking during pregnancy. At the Medical College of Virginia, a researcher named W. S. Stone discovered that some children who were exposed to alcohol in the womb have less REM (rapid-eye-movement) sleep. As you remember from the chapter on heroin, REM sleep is when dreaming occurs. While it is thought to be a less profound sleep than QS (quiet sleep), it is believed to aid in the development of memory skills. Thus, people with reduced REM sleep may suffer from learning problems because of memory deficits.[17]

The reports of reduced REM sleep in alcohol-exposed children are not conclusive, yet they seem to suggest how complex the issue of drug-exposed babies really is. As was explained before, babies exposed to heroin seem to get too much REM and not enough quiet sleep, yet babies exposed to alcohol seem to have just the opposite problem. They don't dream enough. Both alcohol and heroin have traditionally been classed as depressants. Why, then, do they appear to have opposite effects upon the developing human brain? These variations show how much scientists still need to learn about the effects of intoxicants on the human body, let alone the even more complicated puzzles about what happens when intoxicants are used during pregnancy.

Only very recently have researchers begun to consider alcohol's effect upon the developing immune system.[18] So complex is the immune system—that vast network of organs and chemicals that protects us from disease—that how it works has for long been unknown. However, AIDS and cancer research as well as new genetic studies have cleared up many mysteries. We now know that our immune systems use an array of techniques for eliminating any foreign substances that enter the bloodstream. Our immune systems manufacture specially designed antibodies that can attack bacteria, viruses, and other disease-causing organisms.

Not all parts of the immune system are fully developed at birth. Before birth, antibodies from the mother's immune system pass through the placenta to protect the fetus. But once the infant is born, the mother's antibodies start to disappear from its bloodstream. The baby becomes partly dependent on antibodies in the mother's breast milk. Eventually, the infant's own immune system begins to mature and kicks in as the baby is weaned.

New studies show that the immune systems of babies whose mothers drink may be in double jeopardy. The infants' own immune system may never fully mature because of damage to it before birth. Maternal antibodies found in breast milk and designed to protect the infant after birth may also be destroyed by alcohol. In 1991, researchers discovered that short-term alcohol consumption, when accompanied by a low-protein diet, changed the amount and distribution of immune system cells in milk-producing glands. Such results have been confirmed by animal studies. In one study, offspring of mice exposed to alcohol had a lower rate of survival.

Researchers are less concerned about the child's actually receiving alcohol through breast milk. The bodies of newborns have a high water content that dilutes the alcohol, and breast milk in the infant's stomach will block most absorption of alcohol. Still, because infants have trouble processing alcohol, a dose of alcohol that could be eliminated by a mature body in less than an hour might stay in the bloodstream of an infant for much longer periods.

A pregnant woman's drinking is associated with a long list of risks to the unborn child. But are any of the negative effects of alcohol permanent? Current research has shown that the effects of heroin may be correctable in time, but the verdict on alcohol exposure seems grimmer. Twenty-five years after his discovery of fetal alcohol syndrome, French pediatrician Paul Lemoine located 106 of his original patients in institutions. Although their facial deformities had somewhat disappeared, many still had deformed hands and genito-urinary problems. All of them had remained mentally retarded, with IQs ranging from 50 to 75. Lemoine now believes that some of the effects of alcohol exposure aren't even detectable at birth. An infant who appears to be normal may have neurological problems later in life.[19]

Other long-term studies show that children with fetal alcohol syndrome have a good chance of remaining small for their age. They learn to talk at a later age than normal and may have behavioral problems or hearing problems.[20] They may be hyperactive, with poor attention spans and poor motor skills. However, many of the people in these studies grew up in deprived environments. It is not always possible to decide whether these long-term symptoms are due wholly to alcohol exposure or to poor parenting, malnutrition, and other problems.[21] The role of environment cannot be underestimated. Several studies have found that the symptoms of fetal alcohol syndrome occur many times more frequently in lower-income populations than in middle-class populations.[22] What is more, only dramatic cases of fetal alcohol syndrome have been followed. No one knows what the fate of people with milder symptoms has become.

Despite the serious problems caused by fetal alcohol syndrome, some people with this condition do lead productive, meaningful lives. An optimistic article in the well-known medical journal *The Lancet* in April 1993 described a study that found there were improvements, over a ten-year period, relating to facial deformities, internal organ problems, and skeletal problems in a group of patients with fetal alcohol syndrome.[23] Although these problems may not disappear entirely, how much they affect a person's life may depend a great deal on other factors in the environment.

In 1989 Michael Dorris, an anthropologist, adopted a son with fetal alcohol syndrome. He wrote eloquently about the experience in a book entitled *The Broken Cord*.[24] From his personal perspective as a father, Dorris sees the syndrome as devastating and lifelong. But he is not the kind of father who would lose hope. Instead, he realizes that every individual has capabilities that can be developed. As proof of this point, he decided to let his son write the last chapter of *The Broken Cord*. The son's narrative is truthful and courageous. It is proof that children handicapped by alcohol can accomplish much and do have a great deal to offer.

CHAPTER 6

TOBACCO AND MARIJUANA: LEGAL DOES NOT MEAN SAFE

TIME: 1992

PLACE: Ottawa, Canada

NAME: Peter A. Fried

OCCUPATION: Medical researcher

PETER A. FRIED of the Ottawa Prenatal Prospective Study is an expert on prenatal exposure to tobacco and marijuana. The Ottawa Prenatal Prospective Study has compiled information on this subject for more than twenty-five years and is known throughout the world for its precise, accurate data and reliable research methods. Like thousands of other tobacco researchers, Fried is reasonably convinced that smoking can produce birth defects. Yet, unlike cocaine, heroin, marijuana, and other drugs that are illegal, tobacco, like alcohol, can be bought at your corner store.

Tobacco is one of the most tested substances in laboratories and hospitals today. However, without this attention, no average American would ever have thought of tobacco as a drug.

By the early 1990s, over 140,000 infants whose mothers smoked during pregnancy had been studied.[1] Children whose parents had smoked before conceiving and after their children were born were also studied. As a result of this research, the prenatal and postnatal risks of smoking have become common knowledge. There are now laws that prohibit smoking even in many restaurants, offices, and other public places.

When it comes to smoking and pregnancy, any pediatrician worth his certificate is expected to warn pregnant women of the risks. Prenatal exposure to smoking is now associated with the following problems:[2]

1. low birth weight
2. miscarriages and stillbirths
3. premature births
4. learning and behavior problems
5. a higher incidence of sudden infant death syndrome

Although the number of people who smoke has decreased in the last ten years, the proportion of *heavy* smokers is said to have increased. Ironically, this may be partly due to the new low-tar cigarettes. People who are addicted to tobacco have to smoke more low-tar cigarettes to get the same satisfaction. As much as one-third of the women who are of reproductive age smoke on a regular basis.[3] Education on the dangers of smoking has had only a limited success in correcting the problem, because nicotine, a chemical found in tobacco and tobacco smoke, is highly addictive.

Because the Ottawa Prenatal Prospective Study has existed for so many years, it has allowed an in-depth look at the lasting effects of smoking on children. It has confirmed that smoking during pregnancy is related to low birth weight and infant mortality. It has also found that smoking during the last three months of pregnancy has a greater chance of lowering birth weight than smoking during the first three months.

The researchers at Ottawa discovered that some babies exposed to tobacco in the womb have a tendency toward tremors and a decreased hearing response. At one year of age, they score significantly lower on tests of intelligence and reaction time. Although these results may have been influenced by the environment of the babies, there is some hard evidence that a mother's smoking during pregnancy can handicap her child's ability to learn.[4]

Meanwhile, secondhand smoke has become a major issue in the home. If a pregnant woman lives with someone who smokes, she is now referred to as an "involuntary smoker." The same substances—mainly nicotine and carbon monoxide—are taken into her lungs, although in much lower doses. These substances can be delivered across the placenta to her developing fetus. The studies of secondhand smoke are still few in number; however, 75 percent of them have indicated a relationship between secondhand smoke, low birth weight, and higher infant mortality.[5]

Of course, secondhand smoke can affect a child of any age within a smoking household. Researchers have established that there is a slightly increased risk of illness to children who live in households with smokers. However, the long-term effects of constant exposure to secondhand smoke are still not known.

When it comes to marijuana, the answers are not as clear-cut as they are for tobacco. This is strange, considering the wide popularity of marijuana in America. Marijuana is partly responsible for spreading the new drug culture that began in the 1960s across America. But compared to heroin, cocaine, and even alcohol, marijuana's casualties have been few.

This is not to say that marijuana is a harmless substance. In the last twenty years marijuana use has been associated with memory loss, mood problems, episodes of paranoia, metabolic problems, depression, fatigue, and even such bizarre symptoms as the development of breasts in men. Some studies have shown that the tars inhaled when smoking marijuana are even more dangerous to the lungs than those found in cigarette smoke. Loss of judgment due to marijuana smoking has caused car accidents and accidents on the job.

Concern about marijuana faded when other terrifying

drug problems began plaguing our cities. Cocaine, heroin, and alcohol are all associated with greater incidences of violence, including robbery, murder, and child abuse. Deaths or serious health problems from cocaine or heroin are much more likely and much more frequently documented. Because of this, the studies of marijuana are few, and studies of secondhand marijuana smoke are almost nonexistent.

At the present time, marijuana has a mixed reputation. In any discussion about legalizing drugs, this is the substance most likely to be promoted. The Food and Drug Administration has also acknowledged marijuana's medicinal uses. They have approved THC, a synthetic version of marijuana, as an antinausea drug for cancer patients and an appetite stimulant for some people with AIDS. Physicians can also prescribe THC for the treatment of glaucoma. Real, nonsynthetic marijuana, however, remains a Schedule 1 drug, one that has not been approved for any medical uses.[6]

Marijuana consists of the leaves and stems of the female *Cannabis sativa*, also known as the hemp plant. It can be rolled into a cigarette or put into a pipe and smoked, or it can be added to food or put into capsules and eaten. Eating marijuana gives the body a more gradual but less controlled and usually more powerful dose than smoking the drug. Smoked marijuana acts quickly and the level of high is easier to control. Hashish, or hash, is the resin from the flowering tops of the cannabis plant. It is stronger than marijuana and can be smoked or chewed to produce a similar effect.

The active ingredient of marijuana, delta-9-tetrahydrocannabinol, or THC, produces feelings of well-being and sensitivity to sights and sounds. In large doses, the drug can cause dizziness, paranoia, hallucinations, or fainting.[7] As many as 15 percent of pregnant middle-class women have used the drug close to or during the term of pregnancy.[8] In rural settings, where cocaine is a minor problem, marijuana—along with alcohol and tobacco—seems to be the drug of choice for pregnant women who use drugs.[9]

Like all other drugs that have been discussed in this book, the effects of marijuana must be evaluated in terms of the marijuana smoker's lifestyle. Parents who are habitual marijuana smokers are likely to be forgetful and to be poor wage earners. The sense of detachment from day-to-day reality that is characteristic of some marijuana users does not make for good parenting. Marijuana smokers tend to have mood swings and poor concentration. They may laugh inappropriately or get very sleepy as the high wears off.

In addition, there is some evidence that marijuana can cause problems to children before they are born—that is, if the child is ever conceived. Marijuana may cause decreased fertility in both males and females. In animal studies, it has been shown to decrease the size of the reproductive organs.[10] If conception does occur, components of marijuana can cross the placenta or be transferred by way of the mother's milk. Most marijuana will stay in the fatty tissues of the mother, but what does reach the fetus can accumulate in its body tissues, including those of the brain.[11]

Various symptoms have been related to the use of marijuana during pregnancy. In a sample of 1,051 infants screened at Boston City Hospital in 1989, jitteriness was apparent more frequently in marijuana-exposed infants than in those not exposed to drugs or in those exposed to cocaine.[12]

The largest study of marijuana effects was the Ottawa Prenatal Prospective Study that included tobacco. The children in this study were carefully screened to see if the marijuana-exposed babies showed any significant abnormalities. Aside from an unusual thickness of skin around the part of the eyes nearest the nose and an unusually wide separation of the eyes, the researchers could observe no physical abnormalities. However, marijuana-exposed children were more likely to suffer from tremors, to startle easily, and to be irritable. From nine to thirty days old, these newborns also showed some signs of decreased development of the nervous system—especially when it came to visual signals. However, by one or two years, the abnormalities seemed to have disappeared. The researchers concluded that there was no clear proof of marijuana's producing any long-term birth defects. The question of whether marijuana can cause permanent damage through exposure to the unborn still remains to be answered.[13]

Ironically, the dangers of marijuana are much less definitively known than those of tobacco. All researchers agree that tobacco can have a serious, long-term effect on the developing fetus. Yet tobacco, rather than marijuana, is a legal substance in America. Such an irony is further proof of America's contradictory and confused relationship to intoxicants.

CHAPTER 7

THE FATHER CONNECTION

TIME:	1991
PLACE:	New York City
NAME:	Frank Gifford
OCCUPATION:	Former New York Giants football player; sports announcer; father

THE DRUG CONTROVERSY rages on. Most of the blame for the effects of parental drug abuse upon children has fallen on women. This may have seemed logical, for women carry the unborn child and, if they breast-feed, nourish it after it is born. How they lead their lives during these crucial times will have lasting effects on their children.

Lately, however, men's responsibility for protecting children from exposure to drugs is being acknowledged. In 1991 football great Frank Gifford helped the March of Dimes launch its "Men Have Babies Too" campaign. The primary mission of the March of Dimes is to prevent birth defects and infant mortality. In the past, the efforts of the March of Dimes and similar organizations had been directed primarily toward mothers. But Frank Gifford helped the March of Dimes create a new emphasis on male responsibility. He talked about the importance of supporting his wife, Kathie Lee, during her pregnancy and urged expectant fathers to take an active role in protecting the health of their babies.

In the last few years, the focus on the male role has widened dramatically. More and more studies of prenatal drug exposure are taking into account both the obvious and subtle influences of men on pregnancy and early child care. A recent study funded by the Greater New York March of Dimes revealed that almost half the pregnant women who use cocaine or crack have a male partner who pressures them into using the drug during pregnancy.[1] In many cases, the men are both users and suppliers of the drug. A study at Boston City Hospital found that women are nearly five times as likely to be drug abusers when they are involved with a male partner who uses drugs.[2] The same probably could be said of tobacco and alcohol. When tobacco and alcohol are brought home by a male partner, it increases the likelihood that an expectant mother will drink or smoke.

Numerous studies have also linked male drug abuse to battering of pregnant women. One study at the Texas Women's University found that as many as 45 percent of battered women are battered during pregnancy.[3] (Of course, this doesn't take into account another link between fathers who use drugs and domestic violence—children who are abused by intoxicated fathers.)

Drug abuse by fathers is, indirectly, one of the major causes of pediatric AIDS. Most cases of heterosexual transmission of the HIV virus are one-way: it is passed on to females by males during sexual contact, not vice versa. How do these male partners catch the virus in the first place? The majority of heterosexual males contracted HIV through drug abuse and sharing dirty needles. And, as was discussed before, a woman who contracts the HIV virus has a 25 percent to 35 percent chance of passing it on to offspring.

The influence of drug-addicted fathers on children is not always obvious. To understand it, we must lose our prejudices about which parent should be responsible for the child's care. If an addicted woman exposes her baby to drugs in the womb or fails to care for her child after it is born, is the fault hers alone? Should only the woman remember her medical appointments for prenatal care, or should the father be aware of the care schedule as well? How much involvement on the part of the father should be expected during the crucial periods of pregnancy and infancy?

In the past few years, hard medical evidence has linked drug-addicted fathers biologically to birth defects and infant mortality. In 1991, the *Journal of the American Medical Association* published an article noting that males exposed to certain drugs seemed to produce an increased number of abnormal offspring.[4] The abnormalities were mostly neurological, and the fathers were mostly abusers of cocaine. The challenge lay in finding out how drugs that got into the father's body could affect the fetus.

In their search for an answer, researchers injected sperm with radioactively labeled cocaine. They discovered that cocaine specks could actually bind to the sperm.[5] Whether the cocaine was bound to the sperm cells of the fathers who produced abnormal offspring is not yet known, but there is a good chance that this is so. Researchers have already found, for example, that in the case of methadone, the drug can be present in an individual's semen at twice the concentration that it is found in blood.[6] Scientists used to believe that only healthy sperm could fertilize the female egg. Now they have discovered that some defective sperm are still capable of fertilization. Defective sperm may carry faulty genetic information. The results can cause stillbirths, birth defects, learning disabilities, and even cancer. Scientists suspect that certain abused drugs can cause defective sperm. Since new sperm takes three months to develop, experts caution men who smoke, drink, or use drugs to abstain from these activities for three months before they try to conceive a child.

Actual scientific evidence relating male drug abuse to birth defects moves the question of male responsibility squarely into the realm of fact. It's time for fathers to face the consequences of their behavior. They must begin to work with their female partners to protect their children from the harmful effects of drugs.

CHAPTER 8

SOLUTIONS

TIME: 1970

PLACE: New York City, Harlem

NAME: "Mother" Clara Hale

OCCUPATION: Caretaker of drug-addicted and HIV-infected children

IN 1970, at the age of sixty-five, Clara Hale began filling her Harlem apartment with abandoned babies. Most were the victims of substance abuse. Many had special medical problems. But Clara Hale never stopped to think about the difficulties she would encounter when she took a baby in. Word had gotten around the neighborhood. Mothers were arriving, clutching babies they could no longer care for, and Clara Hale just couldn't say no.

Sometimes the mothers who came to leave their babies explained their situation. Other times they just set down the baby and left. Occasionally, they were too embarrassed to show their faces. They just rang the bell, left the baby in front of the door, and ran.

Clara Hale's strong belief in the power of love, nurturance, and patience was called naive by some. Many wondered how a woman of retirement age could put up with the children's shrieks, unresponsiveness, stomach problems, fevers, convulsions, and withdrawal tremors. She was criticized for her simple grass-roots approach and her refusal to use the proper social service channels to set up a "legitimate" charity operation. Eventually legitimacy would come, as would proper medical supervision. In the meantime, Clara Hale never turned anyone away. Her devotion to drug-addicted and abandoned babies became legendary.

Clara Hale died in December 1992 at the age of eighty-seven. By then she had taken in nearly 1,000 infants.[1] Hale House is now a nationally acclaimed nonprofit institution, directed by Clara's daughter, Dr. Lorraine Hale. The cases have worsened since the seventies, and AIDS, which was unknown in the seventies, is now one of the most prevalent conditions of babies who come to Hale House. But public awareness of babies with birth defects due to drugs is greater than in 1970.

Nobody asked Clara Hale to take any responsibility for drug-addicted children. Her actions are all the more amazing because they began without any government aid or charity monies. There are not many women like Clara Hale. Most people don't want to worry about other people's children. Many parents of drug-exposed babies continue to avoid responsibility for their own children. What should be done about these neglectful parents?

Lawmakers, judges, and social service agencies are divided on this question. The case of "Julia," which was presented at the beginning of the chapter on cocaine and crack, shows how bitter this dispute has become.

Julia had lost custody of her child because she injected cocaine shortly before going into labor. After much deliberation, the court finally decided that she had not abused her child. This decision was not based on whether the cocaine injection resulted in harm to the child after its birth, but on the idea that a fetus is not considered a "child" as defined by law.[2]

The decision in favor of Julia came after more than 160 women in 24 states had been charged with abusing the unborn through drug use.[3] Although those cases that were appealed have resulted in charges being dropped, some of the women have received severe penalties. One woman in Florida was sentenced to fourteen years of probation on the grounds of "making a drug delivery to her unborn baby."[4]

The question of whether or not to punish women who take drugs when they are pregnant is a difficult one. Would this also include women who take legal substances, such as tobacco and alcohol? More conclusively than certain illegal drugs, these have been proven to have lasting effects on a child's development. Punishing women who take drugs may not be a very practical measure either. Many lawmakers and medical professionals feel it would further discourage drug-addicted women from seeking prenatal care. Finally, if women are punished, what should be done to determine men's guilt?

Today, most researchers believe that the answer lies not in punishment but in better medical care and education. Study after study has shown that women with little or no prenatal care produce children with lower birth weights, higher frequencies of prematurity, and other problems, whether or not the women take drugs.[5] These women need to be identified, counseled, and given special medical attention. At the Center of Health and Population Research in Albuquerque, New Mexico, researchers developed a very accurate computer screening program for identifying pregnant women who could benefit from education and improved health care.[6] The women were interviewed about diet, drug use, psychological stresses, and other problems. If such a screening system were begun in other health care facilities in the country, birth defects from drug exposure might go down.

Of course, screening and identification are one thing, but effective education is another. Even with all the proper health care services in place, if parents continue to take drugs, the outcome for children may not improve. In an attempt to offer education to drug-addicted parents, the Office for Treatment Improvement of the Public Health

Service is experimenting with two new model drug treatment programs.[7] On two large "campuses" in Secaucus, New Jersey, and Houston, Texas, a large range of services designed to get people off drugs fast has been set up. The programs will have an intake unit, medical and psychiatric services, vocational training programs, and recreational activities. Researchers will experiment with length of stay, methods of treatment, and treatments of special problems, such as depression or AIDS.

Today, "one-stop shopping" for medical care is thought to be the most effective means of ensuring infant health. One-stop shopping means that all medical and social services are available at a single location. These services include drug abuse treatment, day care, counseling, housing, routine medical exams, medical checkups, simple medical procedures, and encounter groups. Mothers also need to be made aware of ways they can check on their baby's health during pregnancy. Techniques such as ultrasound and amniocentesis offer safe means of diagnosing birth defects before a baby is born.

As more and more data about drug abuse and childbearing is collected, certain uncomfortable facts keep surfacing. One study found that in states where physicians are required to report drug use during pregnancy, women were afraid to see doctors because they feared losing their children. The women's fears were not unfounded. Few residential drug treatment programs have child care. A woman who goes into treatment may have to put her children in foster homes. It has also been discovered that black women who abuse drugs are ten times more likely to be reported by doctors than white women, even though the actual rates of abuse are about the same.[8] What is more, problems of low birth weight, premature births, infant mortality, and birth defects occur most often in low-income urban populations. No one can honestly speak of dealing with such problems without taking these serious economic issues into account.

The March of Dimes recently presented some guidelines for dealing with the crisis of substance abuse and its effects on the families of our nation's cities. They have recommended the following policies:[9]

1. **Ensure that there are enough health care providers and enough services.** Services should include parental risk assessment, health education, nutrition counseling, psychotherapy, drug abuse treatment, HIV testing and counseling, follow-up for missed medical appointments, and after-birth care. These services should be available to low-income patients.

2. **Improve outreach efforts to the community.** Women need to know that medical care is available and should not be discouraged from seeking medical care and counseling by overcrowded clinics, lack of funds, language and cultural differences, lack of child care, or judgmental attitudes.

   Neighborhoods at risk for substance abuse and birth defects need to be in communication with health professionals. Contact people must enter these neighborhoods and interact with residents.

3. **Seek an end to the cycle of drug-abusing parents and drug-exposed infants.** School health education programs, family and community programs, and programs that teach about substance abuse and sex education can all help.

4. **Educate the general public about the importance of prenatal care.** TV and newspaper ads, brochures, and community outreach programs should make everyone aware of the epidemic of substance abuse and birth defects in our nation. People must learn about the problem and do what they can to solve it.

5. **Reach out to young people.** Teenage parents are more likely than older parents to have poor eating habits, to smoke, to drink alcohol, to take drugs, and to engage in unsafe sex. They represent one high-risk popula-

tion where birth defects are more likely. School programs can do much to correct this situation. But sensitivity to young people's attitudes is of utmost importance. Judgmental "preaching" is unlikely to help young people.

Young people may indeed be the most important actors in our nation's drama of drug abuse and endangered children. As they reach the reproductive years, what they know about drugs and children will mean the difference between a generation of healthy infants and a generation of infants requiring expensive medical care or special supervision. Young people's attitudes toward drugs and the people who use them will determine what measures are taken to prevent drug abuse casualties. Young people's concern and caring will decide whether today's drug-exposed babies will receive the best care available or be given up as a "lost generation."

EPILOGUE

THE TERM "lost generation" as applied to today's drug-exposed babies belongs to attitudes of the recent past. As was explained at the beginning of this book, early reports on cocaine-exposed babies were full of doom and gloom about their future. Educators, physicians, medical researchers, and parents seemed to have nothing hopeful to say about drug-exposed babies between the years 1986 and 1992. The newspaper and magazine articles of that period, beginning one year after crack first hit the streets, were sensationalist and morbid. They spoke of brain-dead, hyperactive children who gloried in casual violence, had no reaction to attempts to love them, and could not learn or speak.

Then, with astounding suddenness, the point of view of media reports shifted. By 1992, almost every media article had taken an opposite tack. "For Children of Cocaine, Fresh Reasons for Hope," claimed a *New York Times* cover article.[1] The article predicted a hopeful future for crack-exposed children and cited some of the therapies that were now helping them. Likewise, an article in *Newsweek* described a new study that claimed that cocaine did not cause behavioral problems in babies on its own.[2]

At the present time, the media is still churning out articles with the same sunny point of view. It is now the fashion to downplay the seriousness of cocaine exposure and to emphasize the success stories of children who become normal as they grow older. Charges of biased studies, suppressed information, and incomplete data have even been leveled against researchers.

This book is an attempt to strike a balance between the two extremes. In order to create a "story," newspapers and magazines have been known to exaggerate tragedies or overstate good news. Based on the research this writer has seen, it is his opinion that the truth lies somewhere in between.

In reality, scientific research is still years away from understanding the repercussions of the American drug culture. No one understands all of the long-term effects on humans of many drugs. Even less is known about their effects on fetuses. Because of this, our attitudes about drugs and their dangers are often based on emotional reactions and social prejudices. Even this book has had to examine drug abuse from a certain biased point of view. If this book had tried to discuss impartially every drug that has an effect on children during pregnancy or at home, it would have had to be considerably longer. It would have had to take a sober look at the many over-the-counter and prescription drugs that may affect a child's health. These include tranquilizers, antidepressants, diet drugs, antihistamines, painkillers, and a host of others. Such drugs may not only pass through the placenta; a very young child may be given them as medication. Then, of course, there are the chemical preservatives, colorants, and flavorings currently being added to food.

At any moment, today's miracle cure or harmless substance may be called tomorrow's poison. Public opinion shifts as new fears are born. Yet, in the long run, truth will out. As the first generation of crack-exposed babies reaches adulthood, the correctness or incorrectness of our pronouncements will come to light. We may finally sort out the ways drugs can help us from the ways they can do us irreparable harm.

SOURCE NOTES

CHAPTER 1

1. Adapted from Kathy A. Fackelmann, "The Maternal Cocaine Connection" in *Science News*, Sept. 7, 1991.
2. David F. Musto, "Cocaine's History, Especially the American Experience," in *Cocaine: Scientific and Social Dimensions* (New York: Wiley, 1992), pp. 7–19.

CHAPTER 2

1. Mary Ellen Mark, "Childhood's End," *Rolling Stone*, Oct. 18, 1990, pp. 66 ff.
2. "Infants at Risk," Greater New York March of Dimes/ United Hospital Fund of New York, p. 15.
3. Ibid., p. 5.
4. Ibid.
5. Ibid., p. 17.
6. Public Health Reports, Jan./Feb. 1993, "The Dimensions of An Epidemic of Violence."
7. Kathy A. Fackelmann, "The Maternal Cocaine Connection," *Science News*, Sept. 7, 1991.

CHAPTER 3

1. Kirk Johnson, "Child Abuse Is Ruled Out in Birth Case, *The New York Times*, Aug. 18, 1992.
2. "Cocaine Use During Pregnancy," Public Health Information Sheet Update, March of Dimes Birth Defects Foundation.
3. "Infants at Risk," Greater New York March of Dimes United Hospital Fund of New York, p. 15.
4. "Men, Women Different in Mental Illness, Substance Abuse," Public Health Reports, Jan./Feb. 1992.
5. Ibid.
6. Mary Ellen Mark, "Childhood's End," *Rolling Stone*, Oct. 18, 1990, p. 25.
7. For Children of Cocaine, Fresh Reasons for Hope," *The New York Times*, Feb. 16, 1993, p. 13.
8. Mark, p. 25.
9. B. B. Little, and L. M. Snell, "Brain Growth Among Fetuses Exposed to Cocaine in Utero: Asymmetrical Growth Retardation," *Obstet. Gynecol.*, March 1991, pp. 361–67.
10. Interview with Dr. Stephen Feld, psychiatrist, Gracie Square Hospital, New York City.
11. "Cocaine Use During Pregnancy," Public Health Information Sheet Update, March of Dimes Birth Defects Foundation.
12. Ward et al., "Sudden Infant Death Syndrome in Infants of Substance-abusing Mothers," *Journal of Pediatrics*, Dec. 1990, pp. 876-91.
13. Kathy A. Fackelmann, "The Maternal Cocaine Connection," *Science News*, Sept. 7, 1991, p. 24.
14. Andrew Skolnick, "Cocaine Use in Pregnancy: Physicians Urged to Look for Problem Where They Least Expect It," *Journal of the American Medical Association*, July 18, 1990, p. 306.
15. Mark, p. 25.
16. Anastasia Toufexis, "Innocent Victims," *Time*, May 13, 1991, pp. 56–60.

17. Mark, p. 25.
18. "Cocaine Use During Pregnancy," Public Health Information Sheet Update, March of Dimes Birth Defects Foundation.
19. Toufexis, p. 57.
20. Lipschultz et al., "Cardiovascular Abnormalities in Infants Prenatally Exposed to Cocaine," *Journal of Pediatrics*, Jan. 1991, pp. 11–51.
21. Streissguth et al., "Cocaine and the Use of Alcohol and Other Drugs During Pregnancy," *Am. J. Obstet. Gynecol.*, May 1991, pp. 1239–43.
22. "Sizing Up the Hazards of Cocaine Use," *Science News*, Jan. 6, 1990, p. 12.
23. "Newborns and Addiction: A Surprising Study on the Effects of Cocaine," *Newsweek*, April 20, 1992.
24. Frederick K. Goodwin, "Drug Abuse in Pregnancy," *Journal of the American Medical Association*, March 27, 1991, p. 1510.
25. Milnikow et al., "Characteristics of Inner-City Women Giving Birth with Little or No Prenatal Care: A Case-Control Study," *J. Fam. Pract.*, March 1991, pp. 283–88.
26. Interviews with recovering addicts at three treatment facilities, New York City, author's transcripts.
27. Minkoff et al., "The Relationship of Cocaine Use to Syphilis and Human Immunodeficiency Virus Infections Among Inner City Parturient Women," *Am. J. Obstet. Gynecol.*, Aug. 1990, pp. 521–26.
28. "Perinatal AIDS," Public Health Education Information Sheet, March of Dimes Birth Defects Foundation.
29. "Congenital Syphilis," *The Merck Manual of Diagnosis and Therapy*, Berkow et al. (Merck, 1992).
30. "The Dimensions of An Epidemic of Violence," Public Health Reports, Jan.–Feb. 1993, Presented at the Second Annual Utah Conference on Violence, Weber State University, Ogden, Utah.

31. Amaro et al., "Violence During Pregnancy and Substance Use," *American Journal of Public Health*, May 1990, pp. 575–79.

CHAPTER 4

1. Adapted from Susan Sheehan, "A Lost Childhood," two-part article in *The New Yorker*, Jan. 11, 1993, and Jan. 18, 1993.
2. Geraldine S. Wilson, "Heroin Use During Pregnancy: Clinical Studies of Long-term Effects," *Perinatal Substance Abuse* (1992), pp. 224–38.
3. Hazel H. Szeto, and Peter Y. Cheng, "Effects of Opiates on the Physiology of the Fetal Nervous System," in *Maternal Substance Abuse and the Developing Nervous System* (Academic Press: 1992), pp. 215–34.
4. Szeto and Cheng.
5. Wilson.
6. Ibid., p. 225.
7. Ibid., p. 227.
8. Ibid., p. 236.
9. Szeto and Cheng.
10. Interviews with recovering addicts at three treatment facilities, New York City, author's transcripts.
11. William I. Bennet, "Starting Young," *Harvard Health Letter*, April 1991, Health Beat Section.
12. Sara Rimer, "Drugs, then Bureaucracy, Divide Mother and Children," in *New York Times*, Jan. 15, 1991, sec. B, pp. 1–2.

CHAPTER 5

1. "Drinking During Pregnancy," Public Health Education Information Sheet, March of Dimes Birth Defects Foundation.
2. Alexander Dorozyaski, "Grapes of Wrath," *Psychology Today*, Jan./Feb. 1993.

3. "Fetal Alcohol Syndrome and Functioning of the Immune System," *Alcohol Health and Research World*, Spring 1992.
4. Ibid.
5. "The Effects of Prenatal Exposure to Alcohol," *Alcohol Health and Research World*, Fall 1992.
6. Dorosyaski.
7. "This Is Your Baby's Brain on Alcohol," *Science News* 142, 19 (Nov. 7, 1992), p. 317.
8. "The Effects of Prenatal Exposure to Alcohol."
9. Ibid.
10. "Fetal Alcohol Syndrome and Functioning of the Immune System."
11. Ibid.
12. Raju K. Pullarkat, and Beth Azar, "Retinoic Acid, Embryonic Development, and Alcohol-induced Birth Defects," *Alcohol Health and Research World*, vol. 16 (Fall 1992), p. 317.
13. Ibid.
14. Ibid.
15. Jancis Robinson, "Fact, Fiction and Pregnancy" (report on article in the *British Medical Journal*), *The Wine Spectator*, Sept. 15, 1991, p. 17.
16. "Fetal Alcohol Syndrome and Functioning of the Immune System."
17. "Shattered Dreams," *Psychology Today*, Jan./Feb. 1993, p. 18.
18. Adapted from "Fetal Alcohol Syndrome and Functioning of the Immune System."
19. Dorozyaski.
20. "The Effects of Prenatal Exposure to Alcohol."
21. Ibid.
22. Ibid.
23. Hans-Ludwig Spohr et al., "Prenatal Alcohol Exposure and Long-term Developmental Consequences, *The Lancet* 341 (April 10, 1993), p. 907.

24. Michael Dorris, *The Broken Cord* (New York: Harper & Row, 1989).

CHAPTER 6

1. Peter A. Fried, "Clinical Implications of Smoking: Determining Long-term Teratogenicity," *Maternal Substance Abuse and the Developing Nervous System*, 1992, Academic Press, Inc.
2. "Give Your Baby a Healthy Start: Stop Smoking," March of Dimes Birth Defects Foundation.
3. Fried.
4. Ibid.
5. Ibid.
6. "Scientists Discover the Brain's Own THC," *Science News*, Feb. 6, 1993.
7. Ibid.
8. Susan L. Dalteria, and Peter A. Fried, "The Effects of Marijuana Use on Offspring," *Perinatal Substance Abuse*.
9. L. B. Sloan et al., "Substance Abuse During Pregnancy in a Rural Population," *Obstet. Gynecol.*, Feb. 1992, pp. 215–18.
10. Dalteria and Fried.
11. Dalteria and Fried.
12. Parker et al., "Jitteriness in Full-term Neonates: Prevalence and Correlates," *Pediatrics*, Jan. 1990, pp. 17–23.
13. Dalteria and Fried.

CHAPTER 7

1. "The Faces of the Campaign for Healthier Babies," Pamphlet, Greater New York March of Dimes Birth Defects Foundation.
2. "Psychosocial Correlates of Drug and Heavy Alcohol Use Among Pregnant Women at Risk for Drug Use," *Obstet. Gynecol.*, Dec. 1992, pp. 976–80.

3. Ibid.
4. Ricorado A. Yazigi et al., "Demonstration of Specific Binding of Cocaine to Human Spermatozoa," Oct. 9, 1991, p. 1956.
5. C. Ezzell "Cocaine May Piggyback on Sperm into Egg," *Science News*, Oct. 19, 1991.
6. Yazigi et al.

CHAPTER 8

1. Bruce Lambert, "Clara Hale, 87, Who Aided Addicts' Babies, Dies," *New York Times*, Dec. 20, 1992, sec. A, p. 50.
2. Kirk Johnson, "Child Abuse Is Ruled Out in Birth Case," *New York Times*, Aug. 18, 1992,
3. Ibid.
4. Jan Hoffman, "Pregnant, Addicted, and Guilty?" *New York Times Magazine*, Aug. 19, 1990, p. 35.
5. Milnikow et al., "Characteristics of Inner-City Women Giving Birth with Little or No Prenatal Care: A Case-Control Study," *Journal of Family Practice*, March 1991, pp. 282–88.
6. S. C. Lapham et al., "Prenatal Behavioral Risk Screening by Computer in a Health Maintenance Organization-Based Prenatal Care Clinic," *American Journal Obstet. Gynecol.* Sept. 1991, pp. 506–11.
7. "New Concept in Drug Treatment to Be Funded by PHS Agency" Public Health Reports, Jan./Feb. 1992, Office of the Assistant Secretary for Health.
8. Andrew Skolnick, "Drug Screening in Prenatal Care Demands Objective Medical Criteria, Support Services," *The Journal of the American Medical Association*, July 18, 1990, p. 309.
9. Adapted from "Infants at Risk: Solutions Within Our Reach," a collaborative project of the Greater New York Chapter of the March of Dimes and the United

Hospital Fund of New York as well as other March of Dimes pamphlets, leaflets, and brochures.

EPILOGUE

1. Joseph B. Traster, *New York Times*, Feb. 16, 1993, p. 1.
2. "Newborns and Addiction: A Surprising Study on the Effects of Cocaine," April 20, 1992.

HELPFUL PLACES

HOT LINES

National AIDS Hotline	English:	1-800-342-AIDS
	Spanish:	1-800-AIDS-TTY
Alcohol abuse		1-800-ALCOHOL
Child abuse		1-800-422-4453
Domestic violence		1-800-333-SAFE
Drug abuse		1-800-COCAINE
Drug Abuse Referral		
Helpline	English:	1-800-662-HELP
	Spanish:	1-800-66AYUDA
Pregnancy		1-800-238-4269

SELF-HELP GROUPS

Adoptive and Foster Parents of FAS
and Drug-Affected Children
P.O. Box 626
Paramus, NJ 07653

Al-Anon Family Groups
P.O. Box 862
Midtown Station
New York, NY 10018-6106

Alateen/Ala-preteen/Alatot
P.O. Box 862
'Midtown Station
New York, NY 10018-0862

Alcoholics Anonymous (AA)
General Service Office
AA World Services, Inc.
475 Riverside Drive, 11th Floor
New York, NY 10115

Co-Anon Family Groups
P.O. Box 64742-66
Los Angeles, CA 90064

Cocaine Anonymous
3740 Overland Avenue, # H
Los Angeles, CA 90034

Narcotics Anonymous
P.O. Box 9999
Van Nuys, CA 91409

Nicotine Anonymous World Services
2118 Greenwich St.
San Francisco, CA 94123

SIDS Alliance (Sudden Infant Death Syndrome)
10500 Little Patuxent Parkway, # 420
Columbia, MD 21044-3505

FOUNDATIONS AND CLEARINGHOUSES
American Council for Drug Education (ACDE)
5820 Hubbard Drive
Rockville, MD 20852

Children's Defense Fund
25 E Street, NW
Washington, DC 20001

Hale House
68 Edgecombe Avenue
New York, NY 10030

International Commission for the Prevention
    of Alcoholism and Drug Dependency (ICPADD)
6830 Laurel St., NW
Washington, DC 20012

March of Dimes
Birth Defects Foundation
1275 Mamaroneck Avenue
White Plains, NY 10605

National Clearinghouse for Alcohol
    and Drug Information
P.O. Box 2345
Rockville, MD 20852

Phoenix House
164 West 74th St.
New York, NY 10023

INDEX